LEGACY OF FAITH

Legacy of Faith

Rural Methodist Churches in North Carolina

Laura A.W. Phillips

Photography by Tim Buchman

THE DUKE ENDOWMENT

CHARLOTTE, NORTH CAROLINA

Printed in China
Color separations by FCI Digital

Frontispiece: Old sanctuary, Pleasant Green United Methodist Church, Orange County
Facing: Stained glass window, Weldon United Methodist Church, Halifax County

Library of Congress Control Number: 2009943237
ISBN: 978-0-615-34248-1

Design and production by BW&A Books, Inc., Durham, North Carolina

First edition, first printing

THE LORD IS MY SHEPHERD
I SHALL NOT WANT
ERECTED TO THE GLORY OF GOD
AND IN LOVING MEMORY OF
CHAS R MOORE
AND THEY SHALL HEAR MY VOICE
AND THERE SHALL BE ONE FOLD
AND ONE SHEPHERD

CONTENTS

James B. Duke was born in 1856, the youngest son of Washington Duke, a North Carolina farmer. James B. Duke became one of the country's great industrialists and philanthropists; The Duke Endowment is the private foundation he established in 1924. Today, the Endowment works to fulfill his legacy by enriching lives and communities in the Carolinas through higher education, health care, rural churches and children's services.

FOREWORD

THIS BOOK CELEBRATES rural Methodist churches in North Carolina and the buildings that have been steady and beautiful statements of faithfulness to God.

At The Duke Endowment, we have cherished a close relationship with these churches throughout our history. Our founder, James B. Duke, had strong family ties to the Methodist church. His father, Washington Duke, attended a Methodist Sunday school near his North Carolina home and joined the church as a young boy during a revival service. As an adult, Washington attended a Methodist church with his sons. His brother, William Duke, was a lay preacher in North Carolina who built a log church on his land.

James B. Duke grew up knowing the significance that churches held in rural communities, where weeklong revival meetings brought together isolated neighbors and refreshed them both socially and spiritually. "My old daddy always said that if he amounted to anything in life it was due to the Methodist circuit riders who frequently visited his home and whose preaching and counsel brought out the best that was in him," James B. Duke once said. "If I amount to anything in this world, I owe it to my daddy and the Methodist church."

In the Indenture of Trust that created The Duke Endowment, James B. Duke set aside support for the building and maintenance of Methodist churches in rural North Carolina. This lasting legacy still strengthens clergy and congregations today.

Through photographs and words, this book tells the story of generations of rural men and women who labored to build sanctuaries to serve God and neighbor. You'll see that some of the buildings are commanding, and some are small. Some may feel familiar, and some may be a

W. B. Daub, circuit rider. Courtesy of Jonesboro United Methodist Church, Sanford, N.C.

surprise. It was a challenge to decide which churches to include. We had to omit many that were exceptional, but we wanted to show the diversity of communities in North Carolina and include various geographic regions. We only selected churches that have received grants from the Endowment. We invite readers to enjoy the examples in this book—and urge you to explore the many other beautiful churches in our state.

Since 1924, dedicated Trustees of The Duke Endowment have guided our Rural Church work and given direction for our partnership with them. This book, in part, is a thank you to them and a way to document the fruits of their labors. But we also want to thank the many Methodist pastors and congregations who helped with this project by sharing time and opening doors. We offer this book to rural churches across the state to celebrate their important role in the daily life and texture of North Carolina.

W. Joseph Mann
The Duke Endowment

Joe Mann joined The Duke Endowment in 1989 and directed the Rural Church program area from 1996 to 2010.

PREFACE

IN 2007, The Duke Endowment asked if I would be interested in working with them on a book celebrating rural Methodist churches in North Carolina. I jumped at the opportunity, and thus began a long and happy journey.

The book was not intended to be a history of these churches or of Methodism in the state. Such overall histories have been written and many congregations already have compiled and written their individual stories. Instead, the goal was to focus on the visual qualities of the churches, both historic and modern, as captured in a collection of fine photographs. Accompanying the photographs, stories would emphasize important aspects of church history and design. My role was to help select the churches, take preliminary photos and write the narrative for each.

It was a thrill to travel the state looking at good examples of churches, as well as camp meeting grounds, and I encountered many surprises on my journey. Among these were a sophisticated Greek temple at an isolated crossroads, a church whose stonework served as a prototype for that used at Duke University, churches with outdoor worship spaces and one with a dog's paw print in the brickwork. Made of wood, brick or stone, the churches reflected a continuum of architectural styles appropriate to the periods in which they were built. Several buildings had interiors that took my breath away.

Working on this book was a wonderful adventure, as well as a privilege. Not only did I expand my knowledge, but the churches provided countless visual delights. It is my hope that readers will likewise delight in the images and better appreciate the special character of North Carolina's rural Methodist churches.

LAURA A.W. PHILLIPS
Winston-Salem, North Carolina

INTRODUCTION

The architecture of Methodism in North Carolina has evolved over the past two centuries, moving from simplicity to complexity in form, use of materials and style. Many churches and camp meeting grounds from these years remain active, providing a good image of the changes that have taken place over time.

CAMP MEETINGS

In the late 18th century, when Methodist circuit riders first traveled to settlements in North Carolina and to the state's vast backcountry, they held services in homes, barns or other available buildings. These spaces quickly proved inadequate, and services moved outdoors to accommodate growing crowds.[1]

Most of the outdoor sites were wooded with an available water source and nearby pasture. Underbrush was cleared to create a grove where worshippers could stand or sit, and an elevated wood platform was constructed to provide a temporary stage for the preacher. Services consisted primarily of preaching, praying and singing. As the crowds grew, and as people came from greater distances—particularly in the sparsely settled backcountry—services extended for several days. Born of necessity and encouraged by the fervor of the Great Revival of religion in America during the early decades of the 19th century, these services evolved into the annual camp meeting. Other denominations, most notably the Baptists and the Presbyterians, also held camp meetings before the Civil War, but it was the Methodists who developed this form of worship into a powerful and lasting means of evangelism. Churches often were established as a product of the camp meetings. Conversely, over time some church congregations built their own campgrounds, knowing their importance as a method of drawing people to God. Up through the first quarter of the 20th century, Methodist periodicals regularly published calendars and advertisements for upcoming camp meetings.[2]

During the first half of the 19th century, slaves often attended camp meetings with their masters, but after the Civil War, the emancipated men and women were no longer welcome at most campgrounds. Missing all that the meetings offered, several groups of African Americans established their own camp meetings in the ensuing decades. Although their campgrounds were smaller, the former slaves

Tucker's Grove Campground.

adopted the overall layout and building types that had become fairly standard. One such campground is Tucker's Grove in Lincoln County.[3]

The typical Methodist camp meeting ground consisted of two primary parts: the arbor and the tents. Open on at least three sides, the arbor was a large structure with a hewn-timber open framework supporting a massive, usually hipped, roof. A raised platform at the west end held the pulpit and seating for several preachers and often the choir. Facing the preaching platform were rows of simple, wood-slatted pews set on the straw or sawdust-covered packed earth.[4]

Concentric rows of tent lots surrounded the central campground square. In the earliest days, the tents were likely made of cloth or brush, but soon rustic log or frame structures—still called tents—replaced them. The narrow tent lots were sold to individual families, who used their tents year after year and passed them down to future generations. Still greatly prized, these tents have been modified in minor ways through the years, while still retaining their basic appearance. Originally unpainted, tents at some campgrounds, especially at Balls Creek in Catawba County, have been painted bright colors, giving the campground a fresh, festive appearance.[5]

Camp meetings remained popular in the 19th and 20th centuries, particularly in the western Piedmont. Several are still active—Rock Springs Campground in Lincoln County being the oldest—and continue to convene in early August when, historically, crops had been planted but harvesting had not yet begun. As in the days when the meetings provided a welcome opportunity for farm families to worship and socialize, they continue to be highly anticipated times of worship and fellowship.

JOHN WESLEY'S OCTAGON AND EARLY METHODIST CHURCHES IN NORTH CAROLINA

In the mid-18th century, Methodism's founder, John Wesley, became enthusiastic about octagonal structures for his "preaching houses." Wesley found that the octagon form gave the preacher a central position with acoustical advantages and that the accompanying semi-circular seating gave worshipers an enhanced sense of togetherness. There also were economic advantages to building eight walls of identical size, and frugality was important to Wesley. "Let all our chapels be built plain and decent, but not more expensive than is absolutely unavoidable," he wrote, "otherwise the necessity of raising money will make rich men necessary to us."[6]

Despite Wesley's encouragement, octagon churches did not take hold in early American Methodism, and not one is known to have been built in North Carolina. However, his interest in building "plain and decent" churches that could be constructed as inexpensively as possible found a ready audience in North Carolina. It soon became apparent, however, that there was a fine line between inexpensive and poorly built.[7]

A portrait of John Wesley is reflected in a church's stained glass window.

In 1834, extensive remarks were included in the Iredell circuit book concerning the building of churches. "It has been a matter of general complaint and regret that our churches are not built on the most convenient plan, and with the best proportions," the writer, Joshua Leigh, lamented. According to Leigh, churches were multiplying within the circuit. He hoped his comments would guide congregations in planning churches that would present an air of neatness, comfort, convenience and respectability worthy of their purpose. Leigh included drawings—both elevations and floor plans—of model churches of different sizes, which he said, "represent the same general plan and nearly the same proportions said to be the proper model of church building by the General Conference." Although his drawings were fairly crude, Leigh's instructions were specific in terms of basement, main floor and gallery, seating and aisles, vestibule and stairs, correct proportions and measurements, lighting, ventilation, heating and furnishings.[8]

Leigh's suggested church plans were plain, weatherboarded frame structures with a basement, a front-facing gable roof and multiple windows. One had a single front door and a corresponding center aisle, while the other had a pair of front doors and two aisles. In both, the altar and pulpit were set behind a semi-circular rail at one end of the church opposite the entrance. Both

churches were two stories, and both had three-sided galleries. This became a standard form for country churches built throughout much of the 19th century in North Carolina, except that most congregations did not include the recommended multi-purpose basement, and some structures were one-story.[9]

Built in the mid-1800s, Trinity Church in Bladen County reflects a standard design for country churches.

INTRODUCTION OF ARCHITECTURAL STYLES

Over time, perspectives changed on what constituted appropriate Methodist worship spaces. While many congregations continued to build small, plain structures, others began to favor more stylish churches. This was largely the result of Methodism attracting wealthier members and assuming a new role, along with the Baptists, as a mainstream majority among religions in America. As Methodists became more affluent, aesthetic considerations came to be valued alongside the functional. Church leaders began to display a heightened concern for an image of respectability and refinement that would support their role as moral leaders within society. They found that the gable-end, linear plan that characterized the simplest of churches also lent itself to greater elaboration. In the mid-19th century in North Carolina, this usually meant some variation of a classical temple form. After all, there was nothing more powerful than the temple image to convey a sense of respectability, community presence, moral authority and stability.[10]

During the second half of the 19th century in North Carolina, the Gothic Revival style became a part of the architecture of small-town and rural churches. It became so popular among all denominations, including the Methodists, that its most basic elements—a pointed arch, a triangular-headed door or window, a tower—became standard indicators of a church. As with classicism, the Gothic Revival could be expressed with varying degrees of artistry.[11]

NEW PLANS FOR CHURCHES AND SUNDAY SCHOOLS

During the second half of the 19th century and the early 20th century, several developments brought significant change to the appearance and utility of Methodist churches and those of other evangelical, non-liturgical, Protestant denominations. These included the mass dissemination of architectural church plans, the use of the auditorium plan for church interiors and the invention of the Akron plan for Sunday schools.

In the mid-19th century, evangelical denominations began to create church-extension agencies to help fund the construction of church buildings. Still concerned with the quality and attractiveness of new churches, these agencies began to search for appropriate church designs and develop ways of disseminating approved building plans to congregations. Their efforts included producing official and semi-official plan books that were similar to traditional architectural pattern books; publishing articles, reports, and plans on church architecture in the denominational press; and adopting direct mail-order strategies for approved church designs from approved architects.[12]

The Methodist Episcopal Church established its Church Extension Society in 1864. By 1875, through its new Department of Architecture, it had developed a full-fledged system of mail-order church design and stock-plan sales, which it continued to refine and publish in an annual catalog. With this system, a congregation selected a pre-designed plan from an architect's catalog or announcement, ordered it with appropriate features and options, paid a flat charge for copies of drawings and full specifications, and contracted with a local builder. These standardized plans were an efficient and effective way of seeing that distant congregations produced economical, quality churches. When the Methodist Episcopal Church South followed with its own Board of Church Extension in 1882, its catalogs of plans differed little from those of the Methodist Episcopal Church.[13]

The Methodists contracted with various architects to supply plans, but they favored Benjamin D. Price of Philadelphia. During the late 19th century, Price's catalogs became the most widely used denominational church-building resource in the country and were used by the Congregationalists, Baptists, Presbyterians and others, in addition to his targeted Methodists. Published testimonials repeatedly claimed that his designs were the "best and the cheapest." By 1901 Price claimed to have sold more than 7,500 plans, and many of the churches built according to his designs survive. Some of his designs were so ubiquitous—especially the simpler ones—that they go unattributed and are often simply labeled as "vernacular" structures. In fact, some of these churches may be builders' copies or interpretations of Price's designs.[14] Nevertheless, they serve to demonstrate Price's strong impact on Methodist efforts to supply quality church plans to congregations of all sizes.

Avondale Church's interior follows an auditorium plan.

Influenced by theater design, the auditorium plan had become one of the most popular interior arrangements for evangelical churches by the end of the 19th century. As with other period innovations in church design, the promotion of the auditorium plan in denominational publications hastened its adoption and popularity. Many considered it the ideal evangelical Protestant church space. It was used especially by large, urban churches, but was also adapted for small and medium-sized churches.[15] The primary characteristics included a floor that sloped downward toward a central pulpit, seating arranged in curves or angles radiating outward from the pulpit, and radiating aisles. This arrangement ensured that everyone in the congregation could clearly see and hear the preacher.[16]

Religious Sunday schools also experienced a significant change during the late 19th century. Sunday schools varied from church to church, and where they met depended largely on the size of the building. Small churches often had no separate space for Sunday school, and classes met throughout the sanctuary. This was probably the least satisfactory arrangement, as there were no sound barriers between classes and children's classes could neither meet in a circle nor have table space for activities.[17] One improvement was to have a lecture room adjacent to the sanctuary and separated from it by a moveable partition. This space, when opened, could also provide additional seating for church services.[18]

In 1872, the International Sunday School Association adopted the Uniform Lesson Plan for Sunday school instruction, which was later adopted by most major Protestant denominations in America, including the Methodists. It

An example of the Akron plan.

established a common Scriptural lesson to be studied each Sunday by all ages of students in all participating denominations worldwide. The plan called for an entire Sunday school to assemble for common instruction, and then students separated into age-specific classes for further study. Afterward, the classes reassembled for closing exercises.[19]

With the institution of the Uniform Lesson Plan came the need for changes to Sunday school spaces.[20] An ideal model was found in the late 1860s at First Methodist Church in Akron, Ohio. Planned by Lewis Miller, a prominent businessman and the church's Sunday-school superintendent, the "Akron-plan Sunday school" consisted of a central lecture room from which radiated two tiers of small classrooms for age-appropriate group study. Partitions divided the classrooms and flexible doors—folding, roll-up or sliding pocket—separated them from the lecture room.[21]

Since most congregations, especially in rural areas, could not afford a scheme as elaborate as the original Akron plan, architects and builders began devising simpler arrangements that retained the plan's efficiency and primary elements.[22] Countless variations were created well into the 20th century. Even the church auditorium could be designed to accommodate the Akron-plan Sunday school, supporting what had become the shared purpose of the evangelical church: preaching and teaching.[23]

THE PENDULUM SWINGS

At the same time that Methodist churches in North Carolina were embracing the auditorium plan, the pendulum had already begun to swing in the opposite direction. Although the auditorium-plan church remained a popular option during the 1920s, a movement away from the dominance of pulpit oratory and toward more liturgically complex worship had started during the late 19th century. For some Methodists, this meant that the sermon-focused auditorium plan had outlived its usefulness. Instead, attention turned to the longitudinal nave plan often associated with the Gothic style.[24] In the first half of the 20th century, Methodists debated the relative merits of the pulpit-centered plan versus the altar-centered, or divided-chancel, plan. In the 1950s, the Methodist Church officially sided with the divided-chancel arrangement and the associated elongated nave.[25]

A COOPERATIVE EFFORT

The 20th century saw continued efforts on the part of Methodist leaders to see that new churches were both well designed and well built. To this end, The Duke Endowment joined forces with the Board of Church Extension of the Methodist Episcopal Church South. In 1915 James B. Duke had begun giving $25,000 annually to the Board of Church Extension, designating that $15,000 of the money be used to help rural congregations build churches. When he established The Duke Endowment in 1924, it was natural that funding was designated for rural Methodist churches in North Carolina.[26]

Several of the earliest churches built with the Endowment's support were Duke's Chapel in Durham County, Enfield Church in Halifax County and Calvary Memorial Church in Greene County. All three were well designed and well built, representing three architectural styles.

In 1929, the Board of Church Extension agreed to a cooperative effort with The Duke Endowment to oversee the construction and renovation of rural Methodist churches in North Carolina. The board placed one of its architects, H. N. Haines, at Duke University to devote his full time to this effort. Haines consulted with rural churches, drew plans for new churches and for the modernization of older churches, and supervised construction. Since the Endowment urged congregations receiving grants for church-building projects to work with an architect, this program became a vital part of the effort to improve the quality of the state's rural Methodist churches. In fact, it was hailed as ushering in "a new era in church building" in North Carolina.

The architecture of Garber Church in Craven County exhibits a fresh, modern design.

But within months of Haines's arrival in Durham, the stock market crashed and the country descended into the Great Depression. Although the pace of building activities slowed substantially, remarkably some rural congregations successfully completed construction. Within a few years, the church-building program was back in full swing.[27]

STYLE AND APPEARANCE

As the 20th century progressed, more churches were built with brick or stone, moving away from the ubiquitous frame churches of earlier years. The Methodist Church finally had to admit that it no longer built churches that were simply "plain and decent." Instead, those words of John Wesley were superseded by the instruction "Let our church buildings be designed in keeping with the lofty purpose of providing for divine worship, for the administration of the Holy Sacraments and be suited to the ministries of preaching, religious education, and Christian fellowship and service."[28] As a condition of its funding, The Duke Endowment required well-planned and solidly built churches or additions, but it did not dictate style, and by the mid-20th century, both Gothic and Classical styles were still popular choices. Still, some churches built then bore little evidence of style; instead, they were attractive in their pure simplicity. By the 1960s, modernism had entered church-building design in North Carolina. A number of A-frame churches were constructed, while others found religious expression in architectural forms dominated by complex angles.

In truth, no single style of architecture during the last century and a half in North Carolina can be identified as "Methodist." Except for the earliest years, when the simplest structures were built, a variety of styles have been used.[29] And while new churches have been built through the years, many older churches have continued to serve their congregations. These historic structures, along with newer ones, provide constant visual reminders of the long and important role played by rural Methodist churches in the lives of countless North Carolinians.

Duke University Chapel

DURHAM,
DURHAM COUNTY

When James B. Duke gave money to expand Trinity College in Durham, N.C., he wanted the central building to be "a great towering church which will dominate all the surrounding buildings, because such an edifice would be bound to have a profound influence on the spiritual life of the young men and women who come here." For its site, he chose the highest ridge on what was to become West Campus.

Trinity College was renamed Duke University in honor of James B. Duke's father, Washington. Although Duke Chapel was the first building planned for

A statue of James B. Duke stands outside Duke University Chapel in Durham, North Carolina.

Stone for the building came from a quarry near Hillsborough.

FACING: *In the last light of dusk, the tower points toward a darkening sky.*

the West Campus—the cornerstone was laid on October 22, 1930—it was the last to be completed. Julian Abele, America's first prominent African American architect, designed the structure, along with the rest of West Campus and the Georgian Revival buildings on Duke's East Campus. Firms from New York and Boston helped design and construct the Chapel's woodwork, stone carving, stained glass and ironwork, and laborers included Italian immigrant stone masons.

Cathedral-like in size and appearance, the English Gothic building is awe-inspiring. Constructed of stone from Duke Quarry near Hillsborough, N.C., the interior is 291 feet long and the nave is 73 feet high. The tower at the front of the building soars to 210 feet. The stonework that surrounds the main entrance doors includes statues of Thomas Jefferson, Martin Luther and the founder of Methodism, John Wesley.

Seventy-seven stained-glass windows flood the interior with color and depict stories from the Old and New Testaments. The pulpit and lectern are made of Indiana limestone; carved oak surrounds the altar area.

The Memorial Chapel, near the south transept, holds the tombs of James B. Duke, his father Washington and his brother Benjamin. It seats 50 people and is used for small services and recitals.

Duke University Chapel was first used at commencement in 1932 and the building still dominates the Duke campus.

The interior is 291 feet long and the nave is 73 feet high.
Seventy-seven stained-glass windows line the walls.

The Memorial Chapel houses the marble sarcophagi of Washington Duke and his sons, James and Benjamin. Their likenesses are carved on the top.

FACING: *Intricate stone carvings decorate the Chapel's front entrance.*

Goodson Chapel

DURHAM,
DURHAM COUNTY

Goodson Chapel, built as part of a larger addition to Duke Divinity School, stands near Duke University Chapel.

BUILT WITH STONE from Duke Quarry, Goodson Chapel was completed as part of a larger addition to Duke Divinity School. Designed by Hartman-Cox Architects of Washington, D.C., the award-winning building is named in honor of the late W. Kenneth Goodson, a bishop in the United Methodist Church who served as a Trustee of The Duke Endowment from 1978 to 1991.

The chapel's 315-seat interior is designed to support many expressions of the Christian faith and its lofty, open space

evokes a strong sense of peace and worship. Large, clear-glass Gothic windows break the white walls, filling the interior with airy light. From an Italian sandstone floor, the wood ceiling rises 55 feet to the rafters and is supported by trusses typical of those found in many of North Carolina's Gothic Revival Methodist churches.

A choir loft with a magnificent organ overlooks the congregational seating. The 30-foot high organ, which was installed in 2007, contains 1,837 pipes. Its white oak matches the chapel's furnishings.

After a ceremonial groundbreaking in 2001, the Divinity School held its first worship service in Goodson Chapel on April 20, 2005. As a training ground for ministers, it will help shape the spiritual life of Methodist congregations for years to come.

An arcade leads to the chapel.

Goodson Chapel's interior was designed to support many worship styles.

Visitors can find the Pentecost Window in the south entrance of the Westbrook Building, which is part of the Divinity School addition that includes Goodson Chapel.

Cameron
UNITED METHODIST CHURCH

CAMERON, MOORE COUNTY

Cameron United Methodist stands tall in the Sandhills of central North Carolina.

The original wood pews still fill the sanctuary.

CAMERON UNITED METHODIST is a postcard church in a vintage town. Like many North Carolina communities in the late-19th century, Cameron was established after the railroad introduced new economic opportunities. Beginning as a market for turpentine—a product of the region's pine forests—the town soon became a shipping point for Lucretia dewberries, a cultivated form of blackberry introduced to area farmers in the 1890s. With up to 90,000 crates of dewberries shipped each growing season to such places as Richmond, Washington and New York, Cameron became known as the dewberry capital of the world. But even with its prosperity in the late-19th and early-20th centuries, the town remained small. During its largest period of growth, when the population increased from 117 to 218, a Methodist church took its place on the town's main thoroughfare.

Attributed to builders Duncan and Alex Campbell, Cameron Church was constructed in the late 1880s on Carthage Street, soon after the congregation was established. The narrow, weatherboarded building is remarkably well preserved. The most distinguishing feature is its projecting entrance and bell tower that telescopes upward in three stages, each with a triangular pediment decorated with diamond-shaped shingles. A four-sided roof, topped by a cross, crowns the tower and a classical pilaster defines each corner. Tasteful simplicity characterizes the interior, where the center-aisle sanctuary retains its original pews, chancel rail and three-sided apse.

Much has changed in Cameron since its heyday. By the 1950s, both the turpentine and dewberry industries had vanished—now the quaint village is known as the antiques mecca of the Sandhills. Still, some things have not changed. Cameron United Methodist Church has remained a constant center of worship for local Methodists, bridging more than a century of transition in this Moore County community.

Tall, three-part windows line the plastered walls of the sanctuary.

Balls Creek Campground

CATAWBA COUNTY

As part of the Second Great Awakening of religious revival that swept America during the first half of the 19th century, camp meeting grounds became popular across much of North Carolina. The "backcountry" of sparsely populated frontier was especially fertile territory for this movement, as there were few towns and fewer churches but many souls to be saved. The spread of Methodism was pivotal to this evangelistic movement and the Piedmont's broad Catawba River Valley was a focal point.

Balls Creek Campground was established in southeastern Catawba County in 1853 toward the end of the movement. Annual meetings lasted at least a week during August—after crops had been planted, but before harvesting began. Often coming from long distances, families camped at the site to enjoy the worship, singing and socializing that the meetings offered. Farming families appreciated the break from isolated living, and the meetings gave them a chance to reunite with family and friends.

In the 1850s, slaves often attended camp meetings with their masters, and a section of the arbor was set aside for them. After the Civil War, African

Americans established campgrounds of their own in Catawba County. Both McKenzies Grove and Motts Grove trace their roots to Balls Creek Campground.

The state legislature incorporated the campground in 1879. Trustees were given the power to appoint police, who were charged with keeping the peace during camp meetings, from the arrival of the first wagon to the departure of the last. The variety of crimes specifically mentioned in the legislative act suggests that occasional rowdiness had been a problem at Balls Creek. This was not surprising since large crowds gathered there. Specially appointed police and an on-site jail apparently helped, because the bad behavior declined.

Balls Creek features colorful "tents" where families live during camp weeks.

Services are held in an open-sided structure called the arbor. Most arbors that survive in North Carolina have a four-sided hipped roof.

Typical of campgrounds, a large, open-sided arbor with an expansive roof stands at the center of a grove of trees at Balls Creek. It dates from the 1930s, when it replaced the original arbor of similar design and materials. The arbor is the heart of the campground, where all worship services are held. Square posts support the massive hipped roof, and rows of wood-slatted pews stand on a sloping concrete floor. The arbor's only wall is at the west end, where it backs the pulpit platform. A round wood sounding board hangs above the pulpit.

Surrounding the square grove are rows of rustic structures, called tents, which house individual families during camp week. A massive fire in 1956 burned 130 of the nearly 300 tents, but they were all replaced over time, using traditional materials and design. Most were unpainted before the fire, but since then, many owners have painted their tents a variety of colors.

Balls Creek Campground has held religious revivals almost every year since its beginning and its closing session has often drawn as many as 10,000 worshipers. Although not the oldest, Balls Creek is the largest campground in North Carolina, continuing a long tradition of old-time religion.

Germanton
UNITED METHODIST CHURCH

GERMANTON,
STOKES COUNTY

BY THE TIME Germanton Methodist Church was built in 1856, the town's Methodist congregation was well established. Its first mention appeared in Circuit Minutes from 1833. Where the congregation met before 1856 is not known, but conference records provide a glimpse at church activities during those years. Consistently, it was one of the largest supporters of the circuit. By 1838, the church was conducting a Sunday school, and had a well-stocked library. Since an 1836 visitor had commented on the lack of schools at that time, Germanton's Sunday school very likely provided the first educational opportunity in town.

Germanton Church has an imposing, but relatively plain brick exterior. The gable-front building features a central, double-leaf entrance topped by a sash window. A paneled belfry introduces an element of classicism.

By contrast, the interior has a well-developed, Greek Revival stylishness. A refined symmetry begins in the vestibule, where two matching stairs with turned newels and ramped hand rails rise gracefully from each end of the room to the second floor. Hand-built pews feature paneled backs and ends

Greek Revival–style two-panel doors open to the sanctuary's two aisles.

and curved armrests. The focal point is the large fresco of the Miracle of the Loaves and Fishes behind the chancel. Local artist Gerald Steinmeyer painted it in 1993.

Typical of its period, Germanton Church has a gallery around three sides of the sanctuary that originally was used for slaves. A single door from the upper level of the vestibule opens to the gallery, which is fronted by a paneled balustrade and supported underneath by square, classical posts. The gallery's stepped floor holds plain benches with open backs, as well as unusual bench seats built into the wall. Above the sanctuary, the pressed-metal coffered ceiling probably dates from the 20th century.

When Germanton Church was built, the congregation consisted of 49 white members and 27 slaves. After the Civil War, emancipated African Americans

Shaded by oaks and cedars, the church cemetery includes more than 100 gravestones.

continued to worship there, and their descendents maintained the practice until the 1940s.

A cemetery lies behind the church on a bluff overlooking Buffalo Creek. With more than 100 gravestones dating from the 1820s through the 20th century, it includes many prominent family names from the area.

Germanton Church is the oldest house of worship in Stokes County and a rare example of antebellum church architecture—especially of the Methodist denomination—in the western half of the state. Its vibrant congregation appreciates the church's significant heritage and takes great pride in the building and cemetery.

The sanctuary features a fresco depicting the Miracle of the Loaves and Fishes.

FACING: *The paneled belfry adds a strong classical feature to the plain exterior.*

Avondale
UNITED METHODIST CHURCH

AVONDALE,
RUTHERFORD COUNTY

Avondale Church's story has been shaped by the history of the textile industry in southeastern Rutherford County.

The availability of rail service was a prerequisite for any type of serious industrial development in North Carolina. The Seaboard Airline Railway arrived in Rutherford County in 1887, followed by other major rail lines in the next two decades. To take advantage of this opportunity, Raleigh Rutherford Haynes and Simpson B. Tanner began to develop textile mills along the Second Broad River. One after another, the Henrietta, Caroleen, Florence and Cliffside mills began operating. In 1916, Haynes built the Avondale Mill and, with it, workers' houses, a post office, a school and a company store. But with no church, local Methodists and Baptists began holding services in the mill.

Avondale Methodist Church was built in 1924. For several decades, it thrived with a large and active congregation. By mid-century, however, the church and the community began to struggle. Avondale Mill, then owned by Cone Mills, was transitioning to more automated machinery, and the community suffered as mill hands lost their jobs and moved away. Avondale Mill eventually closed, like so other many other textile mills in the Piedmont. With a congregation diminished in size, but not in spirit, Avondale Methodist continued to proclaim its faith.

The church is a large and impressive Neo-Classical Revival style building in tan brick with white wood trim. It likely was designed by Charles W. Carlton, the Chattanooga architect of the nearly identical First Methodist Church

Avondale's curved facade is rich with classical detailing.

in Lenoir. Several other Methodist churches in the Piedmont and western North Carolina share this bold classical design, which features columns across a curved façade with three entrances, flanking pedimented wings and a crowning dome. At Avondale, the original dome has been replaced by a central, polygonal roof.

The remarkably intact interior has a hexagonal, auditorium-plan sanctuary and an Akron-plan Sunday school. Aisles lead from the vestibule to the pulpit area, which is encompassed by a broad, round arch. Each flanking wall has three round-arched, stained-glass windows. The three opposing walls, with the vestibule at the center, feature two tiers of classrooms. Folding doors on

The Akron-plan Sunday school has two tiers of classrooms lining the back of the sanctuary.

Avondale United Methodist ranks as one of Rutherford County's most architecturally outstanding churches.

the first floor can isolate the classrooms from the sanctuary. From the second story, a stair leads to a round classroom under the dome.

One of the most architecturally outstanding churches in the county, Avondale Methodist was built on a beautiful hilltop overlooking Avondale Mill. Although the mill is gone, the church stands as a reminder of the community's earlier prosperity and the tenacity of this rural congregation.

The well-preserved sanctuary has an auditorium plan with curved pews and a sloping floor.

Littleton
UNITED METHODIST CHURCH

LITTLETON,
HALIFAX COUNTY

LIKE SEVERAL OTHER Methodist churches in North Carolina, Littleton's early history was associated with a local college. Littleton Methodist Episcopal Church South and Littleton Female College both were established in 1880 and prospered for some years. Littleton's first church was frame, but with continuing growth and financial strength, the congregation built a larger, more impressive brick structure in the early 20th century. The cornerstone was laid

In Littleton's early years, the center pews held students from Littleton Female College.

FACING: *Folding doors separate a Sunday school/expansion room from the sanctuary.*

in 1906, the first services in the new building were held in 1908, and the church was dedicated on April 25, 1911. The sanctuary was designed to accommodate local members and visitors, as well as students from the college. Every Sunday, the young ladies marched the short distance to the church, where they occupied the center section of pews. In 1919, Littleton Female College was destroyed by fire and did not rebuild. But even after students no longer filled the center rows, the congregation continued to occupy only the side pews. The tradition remains largely intact today—and makes the presence of Sunday visitors obvious.

The church's architect is not known, but since its design is seen in other small churches built then in North Carolina, the congregation likely used a standardized plan provided by the Methodist Episcopal Church South. Congregations often modified those plans in small ways to maintain a sense of individuality.

In the Gothic Revival style, Littleton Church has steep gables, lancet-arched doors and windows, buttresses and a pair of entrance towers. The primary

tower includes an unusual frame belfry with trefoil-arched openings and a slate roof with flared eaves. The west tower is shorter, but no less distinctive. The church's exterior is exceptionally refined in its use of materials, as seen in the deeply corbelled brick detailing and contrasting granite window sills, buttress caps and cornice coping.

From the outside, the church appears to follow a nave plan with transepts, but visitors see a broad auditorium inside. The sanctuary features curved pews, triple stained-glass windows, and a beaded-board paneled ceiling with a rich patina. A recessed room—now used as a chapel—projects from the north end. Folding doors above a low partition separate it from the auditorium.

As the congregation grew, Littleton Church added an education wing in the 1940s and a separate fellowship hall in 1999. As in its early years, the church continues to have a strong presence in the community.

A crenellated cornice tops the church's shorter west tower.

FACING: *Littleton was designed in the Gothic Revival style.*

Wentworth
UNITED METHODIST CHURCH

WENTWORTH,
ROCKINGHAM COUNTY

At the western edge of the state's smallest county seat, Wentworth Church is the oldest Methodist building in Rockingham County. Methodism appears to have begun simmering in Wentworth as early as 1804, when the famed evangelist Lorenzo Dow preached to 1,500 people. The community had a meeting house by 1815, but a clear reference to Methodist meetings did not surface until two decades later. Wentworth Methodists formally organized in 1836 and built a small church that was used for more than two decades. A noted Methodist leader, Numa Fletcher Reid, began his ministerial career there in 1849.

Needing to expand, the congregation purchased a lot on the village outskirts in 1859 and immediately began construction. When the church was dedicated after its completion the same year, a letter published in the *Raleigh Christian*

The balcony pews are like those on the main floor of the sanctuary.

Ironwork angels guard a family plot in the cemetery.

Advocate proclaimed the building "large and commodious, the very best owned by any denomination in Rockingham County."

Wentworth Church solidly represents Methodist houses of worship of the mid-19th century. The overhanging boxed and molded eaves and the bold front pediment reveal Greek Revival–period stylishness in what is otherwise a relatively plain church. The white, weatherboarded building has two front entrances—originally one for men and the other for women—and a side entrance leading to the slave gallery. Above each front entrance and along both sides of the church are sash windows with wood louvered shutters. The most unusual exterior feature is the projecting louvered ventilator at the center of the front gable. A small, open belfry rises from the roof immediately behind it.

The exterior's simplicity continues inside, where two aisles divide plain, boxy pews. Wide board dividers in the center section originally separated the men from the women. Painted wood graining, added in the late 19th century, is still visible on some of the pews. At the front, a railing curves around the chancel,

Board dividers in the center pews originally separated men from women.

FACING: *One of Wentworth's front entrances was reserved for men; the other was for women. The side entrance led to a gallery for slaves.*

which retains its original paneled pulpit. Windows once flanked the chancel, but were replaced by doors when the classroom wing was added.

A cemetery, which includes Numa Reid's 1873 grave, lies in the shade behind the church. It has separate sections for white and African American congregants, and decorative ironwork fences surround two family plots.

When renovations were needed in 1880, church leaders devised a creative solution for funding the work. Members issued fliers stating that the Piedmont Warehouse in nearby Reidsville would give Wentworth church "a liberal benefit from their tobacco sales" during the first week in May. Rockingham County's citizens were urged to take part; the highest market prices were promised.

Wentworth's well-preserved sanctuary includes large windows and a curved chancel rail.

Ever pragmatic, the Methodists joined with the Wentworth Presbyterians toward the end of the century in order to have services every week. The congregations met in the Methodist church on the first and third Sundays and in the Presbyterian church on the other Sundays.

Closed for several years during World War II, Wentworth Church found new life in the post-war years after members added an education wing in 1953. The old church was restored in the mid-1980s, when membership stood at only 39. The faithful remain today, proud of their historic church and determined to carry on in the Methodist tradition.

Pleasant Green
UNITED METHODIST CHURCH

ORANGE COUNTY

IN AN AREA of creeping suburbia northwest of Durham, the 10-acre site of Pleasant Green United Methodist Church is unusually isolated. The church and its cemetery sit back from the road, protected by a large stand of trees. Visitors drive down a lane and enter a world of peace and beauty.

Pleasant Green's story is typical of many rural Methodist churches in North Carolina. After purchasing a two-acre site in 1832, the congregation first worshiped under a branch-covered arbor. A log church followed, then another log building, possibly a combination church and school. In 1869, the congregation built its first frame church, which was replaced in 1910 by a larger frame building that served as the sanctuary until the present one was completed in 2002.

Though no longer the primary sanctuary, the 1910 church continues to be used for special services. The white, weatherboarded building is the epitome of the country church, featuring a front-facing gable roof and square bell tower that projects from the front. Clear-glass, lancet-arched windows fill the interior with light.

Designed by Tise-Keister Architects of Chapel Hill, the

Pleasant Green built a new sanctuary in 2002 (set back on the left), but the congregation still uses a structure built in 1910.

new sanctuary is thoroughly modern, while drawing its design cues from the earlier church. Though much larger than its predecessor, the newer structure sits downhill from the historic church so as not to distract from it. The interior is a large, light-filled space accentuated by expanses of white walls and a lofty, angled ceiling. An angular roof monitor rising from the center of the sanctuary acts as a beacon of light.

By preserving the old and letting it influence the new, Pleasant Green has successfully combined historic and modern architecture. While expanding its facilities for today's congregation, it has managed to maintain a pristine, rural feel near suburbia.

The 1910 church is reserved for special services.

FACING: *The new sanctuary has a modern look that respects its predecessor's design. In both buildings, for example, clear-glass, lancet-arched windows bring in light.*

New London
UNITED METHODIST CHURCH

NEW LONDON,
STANLY COUNTY

On October 4, 1931, when the Methodists of New London celebrated the opening of their new church, nearly 350 people filled the nave and balcony to capacity. The building offered larger and better facilities for worship, but also served as a beacon of hope during the Depression. The large Gothic church was constructed in just seven months. It was one of the most beautiful and imposing rural religious structures in the Western North Carolina Conference, but because of budget constraints, neither the church nor its two-story Sunday school wing had restrooms or running water.

H. N. Haines designed the New London Church. Employed by the architecture department of the Board of Church Extension, Methodist Episcopal Church South, in Louisville, Kentucky, he had come to Duke University in the autumn of 1929 to work with the university and The Duke Endowment to build rural Methodist churches in North Carolina. Haines' Gothic Revival design imparted a sense of the familiar, but also an image of strength and permanence.

New London Church looks today as it did when it opened. Multi-colored tapestry brickwork with cast-stone accents enlivens the exterior surface. Dominant crenellated towers, lancet-arched windows and stepped buttresses between the side windows and at the corners of the towers give the church its Gothic appearance. The front steps rise from three sides to a platform and work with the recessed double-leaf door to draw visitors inside.

Double-leaf Gothic windows flank the balcony and open to stair landings.

The interior has colorful stained-glass windows and an exposed-rafter ceiling. A recessed balcony sits behind a heavy balustrade. With lancet-arched, double-leaf, stained-glass windows on either side, this becomes a rather theatrical area.

The New London congregation traces its beginnings to a Sunday school operated at the Bilesville Academy in 1885. In 1889, the Methodists of Bilesville built their first church, a simple frame building. Spurred by activity at the

With its bold corner towers and brick buttresses, the building was known for its imposing architecture.

An elliptical arch frames the recessed balcony.

FACING: *Colorful stained glass windows and exposed ceiling rafters contribute to the Gothic feel of the interior.*

Parker Gold Mine just west of town, Bilesville grew. In 1891, a mine supervisor from London, England, suggested that the town change its name to New London. The church quickly followed suit. The original church building, enlarged in 1919, served the congregation until the present church was erected. After a social hut was built in 1944 and a one-story fellowship hall was added in 1978, the New London Church campus was complete.

Rock Springs Campground

DENVER, LINCOLN COUNTY

In 1790, a Methodist circuit rider from Virginia came to North Carolina with instructions to form Methodist congregations in Lincoln and surrounding counties. Within several years, outdoor camp meetings—a favorite means of evangelism in frontier areas—were converting hundreds of souls in the region to Christianity and Methodism.

The meetings usually lasted several days. Attendees camped out at the site for the duration, seeking spiritual encouragement and an opportunity for socializing.

In 1828, the Third Quarterly Conference of the Lincoln Circuit voted to establish a permanent camp meeting location within the circuit area. Rock

Frame "tents" provide family housing at Rock Springs.

Springs Campground trustees purchased 40 acres for the campground in August 1830. They selected the Rock Springs site because of its beautiful wooded setting and for the water provided by its multiple springs.

The Rock Springs design was typical of campgrounds built in the 19th century. A large central square provided space for an open-air arbor, where worship services were held. Surrounding the square, small tent lots were laid out in concentric rows with alleys in the middle. By 1830, individual families had purchased all the tent lots in the rows immediately surrounding the square, where they would eventually build rustic structures to live in during camp meeting week every August. Most of the lots in the outer rows were sold by 1836.

The arbor is the oldest surviving structure at Rock Springs. Typical of other campground arbors, it is a large open-sided structure with a massive hipped roof supported by hand-hewn timbers.

The cloth tents that initially surrounded the arbor square soon gave way to small log structures. Only one of the log tents remains; all others are of

The arbor stands at the center of the campground.

A massive roof supported by hand-hewn timbers shelters the arbor.

frame construction. Designed for use by single families, the unpainted tents are built in rows with side party walls and side-gable roofs. Typically, a tent consists of a single, multi-purpose, ground-floor room with a sleeping loft and a smaller room across the rear for the kitchen and eating area. The tents at Rock Springs are highly prized, and many have remained in the same family for generations.

Rock Springs Campground remains a physical embodiment of the Second Great Awakening, the powerful religious revival that swept across America during the early decades of the 19th century. Today, 180 years later, meetings continue to be held every August, making Rock Springs the oldest camp meeting still active in North Carolina.

Campground tents share a common form, but vary according to owner preferences.

Brevard's Chapel
UNITED METHODIST CHURCH

DENVER, LINCOLN COUNTY

As one of the few African American churches in North Carolina dating from the post–Civil War years, Brevard's Chapel is a rarity among the state's United Methodist churches.

Among United Methodist churches in North Carolina, Brevard's Chapel is one of the few surviving African American places of worship from the post–Civil War period. Its known history is limited to memories of older members and traditions passed down through the years.

Before the Civil War, African Americans in this section of Lincoln County worshiped with white congregations at their churches and at the Rock Springs Campground. After the war, African Americans were no longer welcome in most white churches. William George Matton, a preacher in the Methodist Episcopal Church in New York, came to Lincolnton in 1867 to minister to whites, but soon found himself working with emancipated blacks in the eastern half of Lincoln County. Several African American churches established in the area, including Brevard's Chapel, trace their roots, directly or indirectly, to Matton's ministry.

According to church legend, African Americans once walked to the Little Egypt community to worship at St. James, the mother church for African American congregations in the area. The journey was long—four or five miles—so in the 1870s Henry Brevard gave an acre of his land for a new church that came to be known as Brevard's Chapel. Today, Brevard's Chapel and St. James Church continue to share a cemetery.

The diminutive, weatherboarded frame structure rests on hewn-log sills. Simple refinements include shallow, pedimented lintels above the two façade windows and crosseted lintels above the side windows. Wood shingles and round-arched louvered vents decorate the belfry. Superlative sawnwork detailing adorns the façade and drips like icing from the belfry's mansard roof. The fanciful Carpenter Gothic style was popular elsewhere in the late-19th century, but little seen in Methodist churches in North Carolina. The composition as a whole helps make Brevard's Chapel distinctive.

Curvilinear boards and brackets, often with incised and cut-out designs, frame the entrance hood and form a wide bargeboard across the front gable.

Snow Creek
UNITED METHODIST CHURCH

IREDELL COUNTY

A LONG, LOW, fieldstone wall along Snow Creek Road in northern Iredell County marks the location of Snow Creek Church and its 18th-century cemetery. Local tradition dates the wall to 1877, when rocks from the surrounding fields and woods were hauled to the site in wagons. From Snow Creek Road, a dirt lane along the west wall of the cemetery leads southward to Snow Creek Church, which faces downhill toward woods and a creek.

Snow Creek's form matches many other small Methodist churches built in the 19th century.

Two aisles separate the three sets of original pews.

FACING: *Snow Creek cemetery includes the graves of 24 Revolutionary War soldiers.*

The church represents a tangible manifestation of the Great Revival in religion that swept the country at the turn of the 19th century. The congregation dates its beginning to 1801, when an itinerant Methodist preacher wrote Bishop Francis Asbury that he had organized two Methodist societies in the Snow Creek territory where he had been holding prayer meetings. The new congregation flourished. By 1806, when William Sharpe deeded five and a half acres adjacent to the Snow Creek Burying Ground to the trustees, a church—initially known as King's Methodist Episcopal Church—had already been built. It was renamed Snow Creek Church and by 1834, the congregation included 83 white and 17 African American members.

Like many 19th-century Methodist churches in North Carolina, Snow Creek held annual camp meetings in August. The campground's arbor and several hundred tents no longer exist; the meetings were discontinued around 1886.

Little is known about Snow Creek's first frame structure, which was replaced by the present church in the mid-1880s. On Feb. 23, 1883, *The* (Statesville) *Landmark* announced that the Snow Creek congregation planned "to build a

COLE

A fieldstone wall forms a rectangle around the three-acre cemetery.

new church building, a frame building 38 × 50 feet, not to occupy the exact site of the existing church but nearer the graveyard." William F. Bell supervised locals in building the church. By August 1884, the frame was up and the roof was almost ready to be added. A year later, *The Landmark* noted that "the new Methodist Church at Snow Creek—a creditable building—has been completed, and the first service was held in it week before last." But as with many church projects, a few final details remained before the building was truly completed. The Nov. 26, 1886, newspaper revealed that, "Snow Creek is now receiving a coat of paint from Mr. Calvin Wagoner of Statesville. The next thing is a stove and then it will be dedicated."

Except for an added vestibule and entrance porch, the church has remained largely intact. Its traditional one-story rectangular form—with fieldstone foundation, weatherboard siding, front-gable roof, two front doors (now enclosed within the vestibule), and shuttered sash windows along either side—matches countless small Methodist churches built in the 19th century. The boxed and molded cornice with corner returns and wide frieze board lends the church a hint of classicism. A small projection at the rear breaks the basic rectangle and allows space for the chancel apse.

Two doors lead from the vestibule to the sanctuary, where two aisles separate the three sets of original pews. The flush-boarded walls and ceiling give a rather austere appearance, but two-armed hanging light fixtures provide decorative relief. Large nine-over-nine sash windows with cornerblock surrounds continue the exterior's simple classicism. A railing separates the nave from the stepped chancel, which retains its original pulpit and flanking candle stands. An unusually fanciful detail is the wooden segmental arch at the opening to the shallow apse at the rear of the chancel. A carved fleur-de-lis-like keystone crowns the arch.

When Snow Creek members added a one-story frame education building in 1957 and the vestibule in 1969, they worked to preserve the character of the old church as much as possible.

Flame-shaped finials top the cemetery's hand-wrought iron gates.

Abernethy Memorial
UNITED METHODIST CHURCH

RUTHERFORD COLLEGE,
BURKE COUNTY

THE HISTORIES OF Abernethy Memorial United Methodist Church and Rutherford College are closely intertwined. Both began through the efforts of Robert Laban Abernethy, a Methodist minister and educator.

In 1853, Abernethy came to the Burke County village of Excelsior—later known as Rutherford College—to teach at the one-room Owl Hollow School. The school prospered under Abernethy's leadership; in 1858, officials changed its name to Rutherford Academy to honor benefactor John Rutherford Jr. The school became Rutherford Seminary in 1863 and was incorporated as Rutherford College seven years later. The Western North Carolina Methodist Conference began operating the college in 1900.

A new Methodist congregation in the community paralleled the school's development. Jones Grove Church, as it was initially known, was first built in 1852. The small log structure was replaced in 1875 by a one-room frame building that provided a place of worship for both villagers and students. When circuit riders could not be present, Abernethy and some of his students conducted the services. Abernethy died in 1894, and Jones Grove Church burned in 1902. The congregation, which had changed the church's name to Rutherford College Methodist Church, met in the college chapel and auditorium for the next three decades. Although Rutherford College closed in 1933 during the Depression, the Methodist congregation associated with it thrived.

In 1930, workers completed the church construction that had started the year before. The congregation changed the

Built in 1930, Abernethy Memorial remains a landmark in the town of Rutherford College. Its interior features a center-aisle nave with a raised chancel.

KINGDOMTIDE
LIFE
HOPE

A large stained-glass window depicts Jesus the Good Shepherd. Stained-glass windows on the side walls are few and irregularly placed.

church's name to Abernethy Memorial Methodist to celebrate its new building and to honor Abernethy's pioneering work.

The long-awaited church home was a simple, but distinctive example of the ecclesiastical Gothic that remains an architectural landmark in the town of Rutherford College. Skilled Waldensian stone masons from the nearby town of Valdese built the irregularly-coursed native-stone walls that define the church's exterior. A square tower with corner buttresses houses the vestibule and the belfry. Buttresses also flank the large stained-glass window in the façade's center.

The interior features the original pews and an exposed-rafter ceiling with massive bowed trusses. Although traditional in overall form and layout, the sanctuary includes two unusual features. Four large oil paintings set in Tudor-arched wood frames hang on either side of the nave, two per side. Painted by local artist James H. Burrus, they represent Christ in Gethsemane and Jesus the Consoler on the north wall and the Ascension and the Lost Sheep on the south wall. On the back wall of the chancel, surrounding the altar, is an oversized mantel with classical fluted pilasters. A stained-glass window set in a Tudor-arched frame rests on the mantel shelf. Lit from behind, the window portrays Jesus with the Children.

The stone church has changed little over the years and it continues to house a vibrant congregation.

A square tower, with corner buttresses and a crenellated top, dominates the church's façade.

Ware's Chapel

UNITED METHODIST CHURCH

WASHINGTON,
BEAUFORT COUNTY

Ware's Chapel United Methodist Church grew from the indomitable spirit of its congregation. Established in 1890, the church was named for its first pastor, the Rev. Dwight W. Ware. The building was off Market Street Extension on Ware's Chapel Lane, and services were held there for half a century, until limited resources during World War II forced the church to close. After the war, the congregation was reestablished and the old church building was moved to a more visible site nearby. Over the next decade, the growing congregation renovated the church and added Sunday school rooms.

Then tragedy struck. On May 31, 1963, Ware's Chapel burned to the ground. But as a local newspaper proclaimed, "Ware's Chapel will rise again from the ashes." And so it did.

The congregation wasted no time in rebuilding. Elizabeth City architect Edward Pugh Jr., who served on the Bishop's Committee on Architecture of the

At the back of the sanctuary, two walls of jalousie windows form a space that leads to a classroom wing.

FACING: *Wood structural elements and exposed brick create an austerely simple interior.*

Yahweh
OUR GOD REIGNS
Yeshua

Nine shed-roofed dormers on the north roof slope allow light to flood the chancel.

North Carolina Methodist Conference, drew the plans, and officials broke ground before the end of the year. Members and friends of the congregation furnished most of the materials and labor. The new Ware's Chapel formally opened on November 29, 1964, with a sanctuary, fellowship hall, six classrooms and a courtyard.

With its steep, A-frame roof, Ware's Chapel is typical of many modern churches built during the third quarter of the 20th century, although a creative use of light and design reflects the coastal location. Paired windows set on low walls of light-colored brick line the side walls of the sanctuary, but the soaring pitched ceiling supported by massive timber rafters dominates the space. At the base of the rafters, boxed "buckets" hold upward-directed light fixtures, and alternating cylindrical lights and fans hang from the ceiling. Boards laid in a herringbone design sheathe the tall front and rear gables. Both the pews and the chancel furniture are austerely simple, and all the woodwork appears to have a thin white glaze for a weathered, seaside look. At the back, a wall of jalousie windows increases the light-filled space, providing another reference to mid-20th-century coastal architecture.

Weaverville
UNITED METHODIST CHURCH

WEAVERVILLE,
BUNCOMBE COUNTY

A town landmark, Weaverville United Methodist reflects the Neo-Classical Revival and Gothic Revival.

THE ROOTS OF METHODISM in this mountain area can be traced to a visit by Bishop Francis Asbury at the turn of the 19th century. According to tradition, Asbury stayed with John Weaver, a pioneer settler. A log church was built for worship in 1805, the accepted date of formation for today's congregation. Several years later, a camp meeting ground was established, and it became the area's center of Methodism. A meeting house was built in the early 1840s, and before long, a school was added.

Ionic columns line the two-story portico. The belfry, with its own touch of classicism, was added in the 1950s.

In 1850, minister and educator Montraville M. Weaver, the youngest son of John Weaver, moved to a ridge where the town of Weaverville would develop. When the community school at the Methodist campground burned in 1872, Weaver and his son-in-law, the minister and physician James A. Reagan, established a new school that was chartered in 1873 as Weaverville College. The following decade, the school was conveyed to the Methodist Church. It operated under the auspices of the Western North Carolina Conference until 1934, when it merged with Rutherford College and Brevard Institute to form Brevard College. During the school's six decades in Weaverville, its students made up a sizeable portion of the church's congregation.

Constructed by builders Zebulon Vance Robinson and Douglas Conklin Roberts in 1919–1920, Weaverville Methodist Church was a distinguished public building at its completion and it remains a town landmark. The brick church reflects the Neo-Classical Revival and Gothic Revival, the most widely used architectural styles for churches in North Carolina in the late-19th and 20th centuries. It is unusual, however, to exhibit both styles simultaneously. A two-story portico with four Ionic columns dominates the façade and shelters

The auditorium-plan sanctuary has two banks of curved pews.

FACING: *Stained-glass windows depict Biblical stories, including the Parable of the Good Shepherd.*

THE LORD IS MY SHEPHERD
I SHALL NOT WANT
ERECTED TO THE GLORY OF GOD
AND IN LOVING MEMORY OF
CHAS R MOORE
AND THEY SHALL HEAR MY VOICE
AND THERE SHALL BE ONE FOLD
AND ONE SHEPHERD

the three central entrances. The portico's classicism is repeated in the belfry. In contrast to these classical details, the doors and lancet-arched windows reflect the Gothic Revival.

Three front entrances open to a vestibule that is flanked by a small parlor and a stairwell to the balcony. At the front of the sanctuary, a fancy wood grille hides the organ pipes. The two most outstanding interior features are the high, beaded-board tray ceiling and the large stained-glass windows that illuminate the side walls. Stained glass replaced the original amber glass in the 1920s and 1940s.

With the congregation's continued growth, a Modernist Sunday school building was constructed in the 1950s. Today's active membership still enjoys worshiping in a well-preserved church that is strongly associated with the development of Methodism in the area.

The Weaver family helped establish the Methodist church in Buncombe County.

Doub's Chapel
UNITED METHODIST CHURCH

FORSYTH COUNTY

DOUB'S CHAPEL AND its small cemetery stand serenely on a wooded hill, set back from a rural road in western Forsyth County. The present church was constructed in 1909, but the congregation's roots extend back more than a century before that.

In 1792, John Doub and his wife, Mary Eve, converted to Methodism and opened their home to Methodist preachers. John was licensed to preach in 1802. Of their nine children, three became ministers—two locally and the youngest, Peter, established churches across eastern North Carolina and southern

Doub's Chapel serves a rural community in a largely urban county.

The church has decorative wood-shingled gables, an inset corner tower and lancet-arched doors and windows.

Virginia. For nearly half a century, even after John's death in 1814, their home served as a regular preaching place.

When the congregation became too large to meet in the Doub home, a brush arbor for outdoor services was built in a nearby orchard. In 1856, the congregation built a church and named it Doub's Chapel. It served for half a century, until the present house of worship was constructed.

The brick church is similar to several other rural Methodist churches built in the state during the first decade of the 20th century. Although the details differ, as was common with churches built from stock designs, the form and plan of Doub's Chapel are identical to those of Church Plan No. 19A, designed by architect Benjamin D. Price and published in *Catalogue of Architectural Plans for Churches, Parsonages, and Dwelling Houses* in 1885. The interior was remodeled in the 1950s, but it retains a lustrous, beaded-board tray ceiling, as well as its original plan.

Remarkable in a largely urban county, Doub's Chapel has preserved its peaceful setting and continues to serve a farming community. The congregation still includes members of the Doub family.

Cherokee
UNITED METHODIST MISSION CHURCH

CHEROKEE,
JACKSON COUNTY

Consolidating the congregations of four small churches, Cherokee United Methodist Mission Church was built in 1952, some 130 years after Methodists began ministering to Cherokee Indians in the Southeast. The Rev. Ulrich Keener was the first resident missionary in this area in the 1850s. His two-story log parsonage was moved to its present site next to the church in 1958. Although the church welcomes everyone, it primarily serves residents

of the 57,000-acre Qualla Boundary of the Eastern Band of Cherokee Indians. The mission and associated Cherokee Methodist Center operate a thrift shop, child care center, food pantry, counseling service, short-term homeless shelter and disaster relief program. Mission teams from across the country come to Cherokee from spring through summer to help with local needs, and in November, a woodworking team from Tennessee cuts and splits firewood to help needy people in the community survive the winter.

The church is a simple, H-shaped structure, with two projecting wings—one for the sanctuary and one for the Sunday school. Both wings have a plain, pedimented entrance porch; a steeple identifies the sanctuary. Native stones

Nestled in the hills of Jackson County, Cherokee Mission Church was built in 1952.

FACING: *Soco Creek edges the property and provides a setting for outdoor worship.*

cover the church, visually connecting it with the mountains that form its backdrop. Bright red doors add a splash of color.

Inside, artwork makes clear that this is the church of a predominantly Native American congregation. Two decorative panels with intricate patterns hand woven from river cane hang on the chancel wall. A large painting depicts "The Spirit of Christ among the Cherokee."

On the wooded bank of nearby Soco Creek, two sets of benches face a rock altar with a wood cross behind it. Steps lead to the stream, where baptisms are held. The setting provides an opportunity for outdoor worship and reflects the important role of nature in Cherokee life.

Decorative panels with geometric patterns hang in the front of the sanctuary.

FACING: *A large painting depicts a Christ of Cherokee appearance; the painting's name is written in the Cherokee syllabary on a piece of deerskin on the ground.*

Antioch
UNITED METHODIST CHURCH

RURAL HALL,
FORSYTH COUNTY

Like many 19th century rural churches in North Carolina, Antioch's first building was a log structure that doubled as a school. The first services were held around 1830, but a half-century passed before the present church was built. Construction began in September 1881, and by the following year, the church already had been completed, paid for and dedicated. Such speed was all the more remarkable because 1881 was known to have been a dry year in which area farmers suffered crop failure. How the congregation managed to build and pay for their church was a testimony to their dedication, determination and faith.

The church was constructed from bricks made on the site. Built with a sensible, gable-front plan with two front doors, it did not incorporate elaborate ornamentation—but the brick masons clearly were capable of executing more than plain walls. They used raised brick pilasters and corbelling on the façade to create panels, and on the sides they crafted pilasters between each window and a corbelled cornice under the eaves. Doors and windows have shallow, segmental-arched heads, and mortar joints are "penciled"—painted white—in period fashion to define them.

Certain features of the façade are a bit of a mystery. The masons must have been proud of their work, for one left his signature and others left initials. Cut into a brick near the right-hand front entrance is the name "Jesain." Clearly written, it is in all capitals, with a backward "S" and "N." Farther down the wall are paired initials produced by a different hand. No records exist of who these workmen were. Halfway up the center pilaster is the paw mark of a dog, doubtless imprinted while the brick was still damp. One wonders if the masons were amused by including this brick in the wall.

In 1969, the church interior was remodeled in the Colonial Revival style, and an education building was added, both designed by architect H. N. Haines. Probably at the same time, the original open belfry was enclosed.

Today, more than 125 years later, Antioch Church remains a symbol of steadfastness in this rural landscape. With its cemetery spreading out to one side, the church faces a curve in the road, greeting travelers approaching from both directions.

Antioch was built with simple, but distinctive, brick detailing. A panel under the gable peak holds the raised numbers "1881."

Hillsborough
UNITED METHODIST CHURCH

HILLSBOROUGH,
ORANGE COUNTY

Hillsborough United Methodist Church is a landmark building within a landmark town. When it was established in the mid-18th century, Hillsborough was the seat of a vast North Carolina county. Serving as the political, economic and social center of the backcountry, it drew lawyers, merchants and others of ambition. Many buildings serve as a reminder of this important period.

When a Methodist congregation was established in Hillsborough around 1807, its services were first held in the courthouse. After the growing congregation began to raise money to build a church, they purchased a lot on Tryon Street and used a frame house as a meeting spot. On April 4, 1859, the congregation bought the present site for a more substantial house of worship. They selected John Berry, a master brick mason in Hillsborough, as the designer and builder. This was a significant choice, reflecting the quality of building the congregation desired, for by the 1850s Berry had become well-known in

Boxy pews with paneled ends face the chancel.

FACING: *Corner finials and an octagonal spire rise from the church tower.*

Several features align Hillsborough with the Greek Revival style, including the wide frieze board beneath the eaves.

the region. He had worked with prominent architects William Nichols and Alexander Jackson Davis, and learned from them the refinements of the Greek Revival style. The 1845 Old Orange County Courthouse, the architectural centerpiece of Hillsborough, is one of Berry's buildings.

The Methodist church, completed in 1860 and dedicated on October 6, 1861, is a good example of Berry's refined craftsmanship. Its exterior features a sturdy block form, a pedimented front gable, and plain, brick pilasters. The partially projecting entrance tower dominates the façade. On the upper stage, thick

boards with beveled edges are laid with recessed joints to give the impression of ashlar stone.

Unusually tall, double-leaf doors lead from the exterior to the vestibule, where a partially enclosed stair with a graceful, shaped handrail and tapered newel rises to the balcony. In the sanctuary, large windows flood the space with light. The original pulpit continues to provide a platform for preaching to a flourishing congregation.

The pulpit, faced with four fluted Doric columns, is an outstanding interior feature.

Fairfield UNITED METHODIST CHURCH

FAIRFIELD, HYDE COUNTY

ON THE NORTH SHORE of Lake Mattamuskeet, Fairfield is a quiet agricultural village. In the late 1860s, however, after a canal between the town and the Alligator River linked Hyde County to the Albemarle Sound, Fairfield became a bustling shipping center for the county's abundant produce. During the last three decades of the 19th century, the town thrived. Fairfield's newfound prosperity led to a building boom that produced picturesque frame houses, stores and churches. Fairfield United Methodist Church is the most outstanding of these buildings.

The carved "1877" on an upper beam provides the accepted date of construction for Fairfield Church, although it was not dedicated until 1887. The builder, William Walling of neighboring Beaufort County, probably used one of the many architectural patternbooks of the day as a guide.

Impressive architectural features remain remarkably intact more than a century later. Reflecting architectural romanticism popular across America during the second half of the 19th century, the church combines the Gothic Revival and Italianate styles. The exterior's focus is the north façade, where a three-stage tower and polygonal steeple provides the church with a strong vertical emphasis. Tradition holds that that bells rung at Fairfield Church could be heard across Mattamuskeet, North Carolina's largest natural lake. Flanking the first stage of the tower are the two front entrances, each bordered

Set within the base of the bell tower, a wood stair spirals upward to the balcony.

FACING: *The interior's dark wood contrasts with the white walls and ceiling.*

HYMNAL

by classical pilasters, headed by a carved sunburst within a Gothic arch, and sheltered by a small, ornamented porch. Alternating lancet-arched windows with louvered wood shutters and narrow classical pilasters line either side of the church. At the rear, a small, three-sided apse repeats exterior detailing.

The sophisticated exterior hardly prepares visitors for the breathtaking Gothic interior. Features include a beaded-board wainscot and ceiling, and sawn and turned decorative motifs. Two aisles and etched windows with stained-glass borders lead the eye through the nave to the visual and liturgical focus of the church, the three-sided recessed apse. Lined by a blind arcade that is interrupted by two arched windows, the apse is crowned by a ribbed semi-dome. A coved and arched ceiling with ornamented trusses forms a Gothic trefoil.

For more than 125 years, Fairfield United Methodist has served as a beacon of hope for people in this coastal village. For a community often rocked by storms and economic challenges, the church continues as a center of spiritual life—a symbol of faithfulness as the congregation meets new challenges today.

Fairfield's three-stage stair-and-bell tower is topped by a polygonal steeple.

Morrows Chapel
UNITED METHODIST CHURCH

IREDELL COUNTY

AFRICAN AMERICAN FAMILIES have worshiped on this site since Reconstruction. Church tradition says that John Morrow, who was white, deeded the land to the congregation in 1872. In gratitude, they named the church for him.

Churches were the cornerstone of the African American community, especially in rural areas. A school often was associated with a church, and

this was true for Morrows Chapel. At least as early as the 1890s, Morrows Chapel School stood adjacent to the church. In official records, it was known as Colored School No. 2, Davidson Township. The minister or his wife, or both, frequently served as teachers. The school continued to educate African American children until 1952, when the county consolidated its schools and the building was demolished.

Before 1920, camp meetings lasting more than a week were held at Morrows Chapel. People came from miles around to "tent out" on the grounds, socialize and attend four worship services a day. The present arbor is an open-sided structure with pole supports, a gable-on-hip roof and a sawdust-covered dirt floor. Plain board benches with no backs provide congregational seating; a low platform with spaced boards on three sides serves as a stage for the preachers.

Morrows Chapel was built in 1955.

FACING: *Benches provide seating in the arbor.*

The campground arbor stands between the church and its cemetery.

Traditional camp meetings have ended, but revivals held each August include a service under the arbor.

Built in 1955, the present Morrows Chapel is a no-nonsense, brick-veneered structure similar to many built by small congregations in the mid-20th century. Round-arched windows line the sides and a slender, tapered spire rises from the main roof ridge. A combination fellowship hall and education building was added to the church in the early 1980s on the site of the old school. Although Morrows Chapel is located in the busy Lake Norman area, its spacious site retains a decidedly rural feel.

Calvary Memorial
UNITED METHODIST CHURCH

SNOW HILL,
GREENE COUNTY

Built in 1928, Calvary Memorial Church is the congregation's fourth house of worship, replacing an 1882 church that stood on the site. Building plans identify John P. Koch of Rocky Mount as the structural consultant, designer and superintendent. Church correspondence indicates that by the early 1930s, he had moved to California but continued to work with the congregation, planning for the installation of a new organ, new chancel furniture and new pews.

Round windows add light to the balcony.

The belfry rises in stages from a square brick base to an octagonal, wood-shingled spire.The building's refined classicism adds both lightness and strength.

The. Rev. J. A. Russell, pastor from 1923 to 1928, was instrumental in shepherding the church through its planning and building phases, but also played an unusually active hands-on role. Working with a foreman and day laborers, Russell supervised the foundation work, hauled some of the building materials to the site, and personally tore down the steeple from the old church.

Calvary Memorial's congregation struggled to raise money to pay for the substantial building project. At one point, they discussed halting work on the church, but after the women of the church insisted that the work proceed, the congregation persevered. The Women's Missionary Society raised more than $5,000; their methods included operating a food booth in front of the courthouse during weeks when court was in session.

Despite financial struggles during construction, the resulting church surely made the congregation proud. Koch's Colonial Revival–style design, apparently modeled after a Hobart Upjohn design, is exceptional in form and detailing. The Flemish-bond brick structure has large, round-arched windows on either side, topped by round windows or recessed circles. Tuscan columns and a full, pedimented entablature create a temple-form portico that shelters the central entrance. The belfry combines Tuscan columns and pilasters, round-arched louvered vents and windows, and parapeted cornices with urn-shaped finials.

The interior is just as elegant. Lightness comes from white woodwork against cream-colored walls and large windows with translucent glass. Colonial Revival classicism remains strong, with pilasters and cornices lining the walls and windows set within shallow, round-arched recesses. Doors and other wood surfaces are paneled, and elongated scrolled brackets support the balcony projection. A graceful stair with a slender, ramped handrail and spiral newel rises from one end of the vestibule to the balcony.

Hospitality
Healing

The first service was held on Easter Sunday 1928, even though the church was not yet complete. By September, only the interior painting and a few odd jobs on the exterior needed finishing.

On the church campus, one of the most remarkable features is the Sunday school building, attached by a brick hyphen to the east side of the church. Although hidden within the present structure, the building's framework belonged to the 1882 church, which was turned 90 degrees when the present church was built, then converted to its present use. Koch's design for the building was both inventive and architecturally academic—a distinguished example of a Georgian version of the Colonial Revival.

Elongated scrolled brackets support the balcony.

FACING: *With white woodwork and large windows, the interior feels elegant and bright.*

Center Arbor

CENTER, DAVIE COUNTY

In 1876, the Center Methodist congregation built an arbor for camp meetings next to their church. They knew that camp meetings were an important and popular way to spread religion—and Methodist doctrine—to people from a larger geographic area. Camp meeting grounds were plentiful in Piedmont North Carolina in the 19th century, but few survive.

A broad gable roof with German-sided gable ends distinguishes Center Arbor and gives it an imposing appearance. The arbor's dirt floor is covered with sawdust, and wood pews with plain planks for seats and back rests are nailed to board runners on the ground. The raised speakers' platform is separated from the congregation by a solid wood balustrade with a central, built-in pulpit. Three sides of the arbor are open, but the enclosed fourth side, behind the speakers' platform, has wood-louvered windows.

After annual camp meetings ended at Center in the early 20th century, the arbor still was used for other services and events. Before the Depression, these included Christian harmony singing days, an annual fair, and commencement

Measuring 60 by 80 feet, Center Arbor has tree trunk posts; its horizontal beams and corner braces have mortise-and-tenon joints.

services for the local school. More recently, the arbor has been used for church homecomings, revivals, weddings and funerals, remaining part of the active ministry of Center United Methodist Church. Standing in a grove of oaks and maples, it is the only arbor remaining in Davie County.

Center Church was built in the mid-1950s next to the 1876 arbor.

Enfield
UNITED METHODIST CHURCH

ENFIELD, HALIFAX COUNTY

THE MERGER of two congregations, both dating from the 19th century, produced Enfield United Methodist Church. Trinity Methodist Episcopal Church South had occupied two buildings on Whitfield Street when the present house of worship was erected in 1926. Meanwhile, in the early 20th century, the local Methodist Protestant congregation moved from the edge of town to a new building near Trinity. The two churches existed as neighbors until 1939 when a national unification formed the Methodist Church. At that time, the Methodist Protestants in Enfield sold their building, and on a Sunday designated to celebrate the merger, they marched the short distance from their church to Trinity while singing Wesley hymns. The new congregation formed by the two churches adopted the name of Enfield Methodist Church.

During the 19th and early 20th centuries, Enfield was at the center of an important agricultural region in North Carolina where cotton was king,

Wooden theater seats fill Enfield's balcony.

A temple-like portico sets off Enfield's impressive exterior.

and corn, peanuts and tobacco were strong secondary crops. When Enfield Methodist Church was built in 1926, the congregation—blessed with prosperity from agriculture—was able to construct an unusually fine building.

H. M. King, a prominent Kentucky architect, designed the stately church in the Neo-Classical Revival style. White detailing adds visual appeal to the exterior's red brick walls. The focal point is the temple-like, pedimented Doric portico, reached by a monumental flight of front steps. The richly molded, two-part cornice that wraps around the building and the imposing front entrance add to its classicism.

Inside, dark woodwork plays against cream-colored stuccoed walls. The chancel is noteworthy for its heavily turned communion rail, paneled choir loft, and broad arch that frames the organ pipes. The well-designed interior also features a box-beamed ceiling and a staircase with paneled detailing that rises to the balcony.

Much has changed in the agricultural economy of North Carolina, but Enfield United Methodist survives as a reminder of the region's prosperity and gives witness to the faithfulness of generations.

Round-arched stained-glass windows light the sanctuary.

Grassy Creek UNITED METHODIST CHURCH

GRASSY CREEK,
ASHE COUNTY

NESTLED IN ONE of the most beautiful rural landscapes in northwestern North Carolina, Grassy Creek is a small community whose economy has been tied to two centuries of cattle farming. It lies so close to Virginia that the social and economic activities of its citizens ignore the state line.

The Grassy Creek congregation was organized before 1900 and met for a

time in Virginia. Even after 1904, when the present church was built across the state line, it was aligned with Virginia Methodists until 1925.

The Methodists situated their frame church on a knoll overlooking the creek valley. E. L. Robbins, who also built the Grayson County Courthouse in Virginia, signed on as builder. The Gothic Revival structure has lancet-arched doors and windows and a corner tower that holds the belfry. Round-cut wood shingles cover the front gable and the second stage of the tower, providing a textural contrast to the plain weatherboards on the rest of the exterior.

In northwestern North Carolina, Grassy Creek Church is bordered by Christmas tree farms.

HYMNAL

Colorful stained-glass windows brighten the wood walls.

Inside, the sanctuary is covered with wood-stained beaded boards, which give a rich, warm feeling. The ceiling has square panels with beaded boards that alternate direction from one panel to the next. Each stained-glass window has a different design. One window includes three Masonic symbols; tradition says that after Masons were dismissed from the Baptist church, they joined the Methodists.

From its lone hilltop site, Grassy Creek Church serves as a beacon to the area, while devoted members make sure it maintains an active role in daily life.

First UNITED METHODIST CHURCH

MURPHY, CHEROKEE COUNTY

The vestibule opens to a six-sided sanctuary.

MURPHY WAS INCORPORATED in 1851, two decades after it was first settled. A Methodist minister was assigned to the town in 1858, and seven years later, Joshua Harshaw donated land and a meeting house to the fledgling congregation. Harshaw Chapel still stands, but as the town grew, so did the number of Methodists, and eventually the congregation needed a larger building. The present church was constructed in 1922.

ABIDE
IN
ME

A decorative pressed metal ceiling contrasts with the sanctuary's warm wood paneling.

First Church has a bold, Neo-Classical Revival style, with white wood detailing that contrasts with warm, red-brick walls. The exterior focal point is a curved façade with two-story Doric columns that rise to a full entablature and separate the three entrances and second-story round-arched windows. A tall flight of curved steps leads to the entrances, and the whole is crowned by a round dome.

The entrance vestibule opens to a six-sided, auditorium-plan sanctuary with an Akron-plan Sunday school wrapping around the rear sides. Three banks of curved pews face the pulpit, which is framed by a large, splayed, round arch. Flanking walls feature a trio of two-story, stained-glass windows. Wood paneling in the sanctuary and Sunday school contrasts with plastered walls and a white ceiling of decorative pressed metal. Two tiers of classrooms are divided by posts and half walls; one retains wooden accordion doors. Classroom pews face the sanctuary. Stairs lead to the dome, which houses the men's classroom.

Although the architect of this outstanding building is not known, it may have been Chattanooga's Charles W. Carlton, who designed the nearly identical First Methodist Church in Lenoir. Other Methodist churches in Piedmont and Western North Carolina—including Avondale in Rutherford County, First Church in Lincolnton, and Green Street and the former Burkhead churches in Winston-Salem—display the same design. All were likely Carlton's work or copied from churches he designed.

Today, Murphy's First United Methodist Church still has a large and vibrant congregation. Reflecting its important role in the community, the church commands a prominent downtown location in direct line with the town square.

Two-story Doric columns mark First Church's curved entrance. Pedimented wings on a raised basement flank the façade.

Oxford UNITED METHODIST CHURCH

OXFORD,
GRANVILLE COUNTY

A patterned slate roof tops Oxford's red brick.

When Oxford Methodist Church began holding services in 1902, the local *Public Ledger* described the new structure as "a beautiful modern brick edifice, one which would do credit to a city." The church remains one of the most striking and ornate buildings in Granville County.

The Gothic Revival design with Queen Anne-style influences is attributed to prominent German-born architect Charles E. Hartge of Raleigh.

The sanctuary features a paneled ceiling and three-part stained-glass windows on the east and west sides.

Organ pipes gleam in the chancel.

FACING: *Exterior details include a belfry surrounded by arched openings and small decorative gables.*

The asymmetrical exterior shows a variety of materials, forms and details, including brickwork enlivened by heavily corbeled and molded features. The College Street façade boasts two complex entrance towers. Both have a square first stage and a polygonal second stage with three-step buttresses. From there, the north tower soars upward with a cylindrical shaft, ending in a polygonal fourth stage belfry.

The lofty interior is just as richly detailed. The sanctuary follows an auditorium plan with entrances at the four corners. A beaded-board, coved cornice with applied sawnwork ornamentation separates the white walls from the cruciform-shaped ceiling. A 1929 remodeling created the main McClanahan Street entrance and removed the balcony, although the ironwork columns that supported it still remain.

The 1902 church was the fourth for the Methodist congregation in Oxford. The first, built in 1822, was also the first church of any denomination in town. It was replaced in 1836 by the second church, which served the congregation until 1867, when a third structure was built. By the end of the century, with more than 300 members, the congregation once again needed more room. This time, they built a much larger brick church—clearly a building of permanence—that continues to serve the congregation more than 100 years later.

Whitakers

UNITED METHODIST CHURCH

WHITAKERS, NASH COUNTY

In the Whitakers community, two branches of Methodism followed relatively parallel paths of development before the 1939 national unification that established the Methodist Church.

Whitakers Methodist Protestant Church began as an outgrowth of the 1860s Old Temple Church, which stood just outside the community. The congregation built a frame church on Cutchin Street, which served them until lightning severely damaged the building in 1915. After meeting for a while in a movie theater, church members purchased a lot at the corner of New and Pippen streets, and in 1917 built a brick structure on the site. A large stained-glass window that survived the storm was installed on the Pippen Street side of the new building.

Meanwhile, the congregation of Whitakers Methodist Episcopal Church South built a church for themselves in 1887 at Pippen and White streets. The congregation worshiped there for half a century, until a fire in 1937. For a year afterward, they then met in the Methodist Protestant building.

After the two congregations began discussing unification, the Methodist Protestants agreed to provide the church building and parsonage, while the Methodist Episcopal Church South furnished a pastor and more than half of his salary. Whitakers Methodist Church was established a year ahead of national unification.

Roll-up doors enclose a Sunday school assembly room that can also serve as extra sanctuary seating.

Today, the church continues to occupy the 1917 late Gothic Revival–style brick building. Simple in detail, it features Tudor-arched doors and windows rather than lancet-arched openings. The two street facades are nearly identical and meet at a corner entrance/bell tower.

The sanctuary follows an auditorium plan with curved pews and a center aisle that runs diagonally from the corner entrance tower. Recessed behind broad segmental arches, three walls are filled with large stained-glass windows.

A center aisle leads to the round, Colonial Revival–style chancel.

Whitakers' corner tower has doors that open onto Pippen and New streets.

Roll-up doors on the fourth wall separate the sanctuary and the small Akron-plan Sunday school, where individual classrooms surround an assembly room.

In 1952, the congregation purchased a lot on Pippen Street adjoining the church and later built a one-story brick education building. Designed to complement the 1917 church, it has a Tudor-arched front entrance with flanking pilasters and a stepped-parapet cornice that nearly duplicates the secondary side entrances of the church.

Bethel UNITED METHODIST CHURCH

CASWELL COUNTY

Bethel Church began in the 19th century as a non-denominational house of worship used primarily by Primitive Baptists and Methodists. It was abandoned in 1874, being both dilapidated and only occasionally used. A decade later, however, the Methodists reclaimed the building, enlarging and remodeling it. Typical of rural churches built then, it was a plain, white, weatherboarded structure with an entrance in the gable end and windows along both sides. The church stood on the site of the present cemetery.

By 1918, the growing congregation had acquired a lot across the road, and a brick structure was soon erected. It was anything *but* typical. The Greek temple design is unexpected, if not visually startling, at this sparsely settled crossroads. While Neo-Classical Revival buildings were popular during the early 20th century, rarely did they adopt such a strictly Greek vocabulary.

The focal point of the tan brick building is the bold temple portico. Designed in the Greek Doric order, it features heavy fluted columns and a full entablature with a plain architrave, a triglyph-and-metope frieze and a pedimented cornice. Almost hidden from view, the recessed portico ceiling has decorative paneling surrounded by a dentil border. A tile roof furthers the temple effect. The fact that all these features appear to be metal, rather than stone, wood, or terra cotta, is surprising.

A tall, double-leaf entrance opens to the sanctuary, where dark-stained woodwork—including a grid of ceiling beams—contrasts

Bethel's Greek temple design stands out in north central North Carolina.

with the cream-colored stuccoed walls and ceiling. A broad arch flanked by two smaller arches separates the nave from the chancel. Stained-glass windows were added in the 1950s and the church achieved its present size and appearance with later additions.

Like a rock of faith watching over this rural crossroads, Bethel Church continues to provide an image of strength and stability, as it did nearly a century earlier.

With a three-step base, the temple portico is designed in the Greek Doric order.

FACING: *Dark-stained woodwork accents the walls and ceiling.*

Camp Ground
UNITED METHODIST CHURCH

FAYETTEVILLE,
CUMBERLAND COUNTY

Camp Ground's white interior typifies the period.

CAMP GROUND CHURCH'S name reflects an early history that was typical of many rural churches in North Carolina and was essential to the spread of Methodism. As early as 1800, a Methodist church was established in nearby Fayetteville, but it had little impact on farm families who lived in the expansive countryside. Camp meetings, or revivals, became a way to spread religion to that scattered population and drew people from remote rural areas for preaching, singing, prayer and fellowship.

Exactly when camp meetings began on the knoll overlooking Beaver Creek is not known, although records suggest they were being held at least by 1834. During the early years, a large brush arbor served as the place of worship; a log church and a graveyard were added later. By 1862, a new church had been built, although—probably due to the Civil War—more than a decade passed before all the detailing and furnishings were completed. In 1874, Charge Pastor W. S. Griffin finally reported that, "At the Camp Ground we have a most excellent Church finished off in good style."

Although churches of this type were once common in rural areas, relatively few survive.

Camp Ground Church's exterior epitomizes the basic form of the typical

Two sets of steep stairs at the rear corners of the church lead to the gallery.

FACING: *Because of the sanctuary's size, two-story chamfered posts support a central beam that runs the length of the church. Posts also support the gallery.*

mid-19th-century rural Methodist building: a simple, blocky, rectangle with white-painted weatherboard siding, a front-facing gable roof, entrances with multi-pane transoms, and sash windows surrounding the whole. In Camp Ground's case, the pedimented front gable provides a hint of the Greek Revival. Churches of this type were built with one or two stories, and although they were once a common feature of the rural landscape, relatively few survive.

The white interior also is typical of this period, but it exhibits considerably more refinement than the exterior. The sanctuary has two side aisles, a raised chancel and a three-sided gallery. The decorative pressed-metal ceiling is an addition, as is the vestibule, which was created by partitioning off the rear of the sanctuary. Handsome pine pews with graceful curved arms fill the first floor; in the center section, the pews are made of boards that are 15 inches wide and 15 feet long. In the gallery, boxed pews sit on a steeply tilted floor.

A century after Camp Ground Church was built, its congregation had grown to the point that new facilities were necessary. A new sanctuary was built in the late 1960s, followed by substantial wings for the church school on one side and the fellowship hall and offices on the other. The old church was not demolished, but moved to the rear of the grounds adjacent to the cemetery, where the congregation continues to use it for special services.

Tucker's Grove Campground

LINCOLN COUNTY

IN HIS JOURNALS, Bishop Francis Asbury often voiced his great concern for the plight of slaves in the American South. "Who will take the pains," he wrote in 1809, "to lead them into the way of salvation, and watch over them that they may not stray, but the Methodists?" In North Carolina, many Methodist churches allowed slaves to attend worship services with their masters, usually seated separately in a rear or three-sided gallery above the main floor of the sanctuary. Slaves also were allowed to attend some camp meetings, such as Rock Springs in Lincoln County and Balls Creek in Catawba County. After

The arbor at Tucker's Grove has a sawdust-covered clay floor; the pulpit stands on a raised platform.

the Civil War, however, emancipated slaves often were no longer welcome in white churches and campgrounds so they began to establish their own places of worship.

Although some tradition claims that Tucker's Grove Campground was started during the first half of the 19th century, this seems unlikely since slaves were not allowed to congregate in large numbers. It is more likely that Tucker's Grove began in the 1870s, like Mott's Grove and McKenzie's Grove campgrounds in neighboring Catawba County. A campground monument marks the date as 1874 and it was later in the decade that Mary E. Tucker gave the oak grove site to the trustees.

The arbor, where worship services are held, stands at the campground's center. The structure's roof is supported by a framework of hewn timbers that are mortised, tenoned and locked in place by large wooden pegs. Unhewn poles support the eaves, which sweep so low that warning flags have been hung from them. Sawdust covers the hard-packed clay floor. Rows of pine benches face the pulpit, which stands on a low platform at the front.

Tucker's Grove follows traditional plans and building forms of earlier campgrounds.

A framework of hewn timbers supports the massive roof.

Rustic wood tents surround the arbor.

More than 100 tents with common side walls and shallow gable roofs form a square around the arbor. Fires have destroyed some of the tents, but they continue to be rebuilt in the same way. Owned by individual families, they become a home away from home during camp weeks every August.

As at other campgrounds, meeting time at Tucker's Grove remains an important annual event. Participants enjoy extended visits with old friends and family, who often come from far away to attend. This religious and social tradition has continued for more than 125 years and promises to extend well into the future.

Duke's Chapel
UNITED METHODIST CHURCH

DURHAM, DURHAM COUNTY

In 1840, William "Uncle Billy" Duke built a log church known as Mount Hebron on his land. A Methodist lay preacher and the oldest brother of tobacco magnate Washington Duke, he greatly influenced the religious life of the entire Duke family, while advancing Methodism in the Durham area. Two years after Billy Duke's death in 1883, the Mount Hebron congregation built a frame house of worship on Old Oxford Highway, about a mile from the original church. They named it Duke's Chapel to honor their founding father. This was the first institution of any type to carry the Duke name.

By the early 1920s, the need for a larger church had become obvious and construction plans were underway by 1925. The prominent Philadelphia architectural firm of Horace Trumbauer, which designed the buildings at Duke University, prepared the plans and specifications. It is likely that Julian Abele, Trumbauer's chief designer and America's first well-known African American architect, designed Duke's Chapel, since he also designed the university buildings. The E. H. Clement Company of Charlotte signed on as contractor. Since the architect and the contractor were based elsewhere, Duke University donated the services of its resident architect and construction engineer to oversee the onsite work. The cornerstone was laid in 1926, and the formal opening followed on July 24, 1927.

Church tradition claims that Duke's Chapel served as an experimental prototype for the stonework that was to be used on the Duke campus. With its broad range of colors, the stone came from a university-owned quarry near Hillsborough. The type of broad, flat

The stone used for Duke's Chapel came from a quarry near Hillsborough.

mortar joints that distinguishes the university stonework also was used first at Duke's Chapel.

As the building neared completion, the *Durham Morning Herald* proclaimed it to be "the finest rural church in North Carolina." The L-shaped stone building with entrance tower resembles an English country church. It features pointed-arched primary doors and windows with decorative stone surrounds, buttresses with stone caps along either side wall, and flared eaves. The quiet coolness of

Duke's Chapel has served as a training ground for ministerial students at Duke University's School of Religion.

the center-aisle nave sanctuary continues the medieval Gothic feel. The ceiling, with its round-arched trusses and original hanging light fixtures, is especially impressive. At the rear, a small balcony is set within a pointed arch. Colorful stained glass was installed in 1947.

At the request of Benjamin Duke, the church served as a training ground for ministerial students at Duke University's School of Religion, a tradition that soon expanded to other rural Methodist churches in the state. In its early years, Duke's Chapel doubled as the parsonage, since the congregation was unable to pay for a separate building. Except on Sunday mornings, the first-floor classrooms served as the living room, dining room and kitchen; the bedrooms

Thick, white-plastered walls fill the space between the beaded-board wainscot and ceiling.

The colorful stained glass of the side and chancel windows was installed in 1947.

were upstairs. The church rented a nearby house in 1941, but Duke's Chapel built its own parsonage a few years later using stones from the same quarry.

When the education building was constructed on the north side of Duke's Chapel in the late 1960s, it was a thoroughly modern, two-story brick and glass building. The architects, Hackney and Knott of Durham, positioned the new building toward the back of the church, so as not to detract from the earlier building, and visually linked it with stonework.

Weldon
UNITED METHODIST CHURCH

WELDON, HALIFAX COUNTY

Crews remodeled the sanctuary in the 1950s, but Weldon's original stained-glass windows remain.

THE CONSTRUCTION OF the Roanoke Canal in the early 19th century and the arrival of North Carolina's first four railroads established Weldon as a regionally important transportation hub. With growing affluence, the town produced many architecturally notable buildings. Weldon United Methodist Church holds a prominent place among these.

Methodists in Weldon established the town's first religious congregation in 1845. By the turn of the 20th century, the town's prospects for a vibrant future encouraged the Methodists to erect a remarkable house of worship, their third, at Washington Avenue and East Fifth Street. The fact that, in 1910, they were able to hire the prominent Charlotte architectural firm of Wheeler and Stern attests to the congregation's prosperity.

Weldon was built in 1910, but the sanctuary was later enlarged.

WELDON
UNITED METHODIST CHURCH
11 00 AM
WELCOME
OPEN DOORS

The exterior features two soaring towers and a wealth of brick corbelling.

Throughout the construction project, *The Roanoke News* gave frequent reports on the building's progress. On July 14, the brick walls were nearly complete. On September 15, the slate roof was being installed. Work was underway on the steeples and plaster on October 6 and, on Thanksgiving Day, the cornerstone was laid. Less than two months later, the first services were held.

In majestic Gothic Revival style, the structure is dominated by a pair of dramatic towers topped by octagonal spires that rise above crenellated parapets. Other detailing includes Gothic-arched doors and windows, a metal coved cornice and a rich collection of brick corbelling.

As one of the main churches in town, Weldon Methodist played an active role in the community. Perhaps the most unusual event took place in 1931, when a tonsil clinic was held in the church basement and 48 children had their tonsils removed.

Starting in September 1957, the church underwent a major, year-long building program. Crews enlarged and remodeled the sanctuary interior, while retaining the magnificent original stained-glass windows. A Neo-Gothic-style brick education building, designed by the Wilson architectural firm of Charles C. Benton and Sons, was built on the church's northeast side.

Weldon United Methodist Church reflects the phenomenal changes brought by the railroad in North Carolina during the 19th and early 20th centuries. The canal is gone and the railroads no longer play a large part in Weldon's economy, but the church survives as a witness to the congregation's hopes and dreams.

Union Grove
UNITED METHODIST CHURCH

ORANGE COUNTY

FOR THE FIRST several decades after Union Grove Church was organized in 1846, the congregation met in a log school house. Circuit riders led worship services whenever they could; in 1869, services began to be held once a month. Two years later, the congregation acquired five acres for a cemetery and a new, one-room frame church. Like many rural Methodist churches, Union Grove held an annual revival during the first week in August when crops had been planted, but the harvest had not yet begun.

On September 29, 1946, nearly 300 people gathered to celebrate the church's centennial and lay the cornerstone for a new house of worship next to the 1871 building. With its native-stone veneer and steeply pitched roof, the church would look at home in the English countryside. Later additions were all made with the same native stone. The sanctuary was remodeled in the Colonial Revival style in 1972, but the pine pews from the 1871 church were refinished for continued use.

Union Grove's sanctuary was remodeled in the Colonial Revival style in 1972.

Although close to Chapel Hill, Union Grove's site is remarkably rural. The church is set back from the road on 22 wooded acres with a cemetery on one side and a parsonage on the other. A beautiful new fellowship hall stands behind the church on a large field that can be used for sports. An opening in the woods takes visitors to an outdoor worship space next to a spring and small stream. A foot bridge leads to plain benches that rise in two rows with the hillside. Behind the benches stands a wood cross made of rough poles.

Union Grove's exterior includes a gabled vestibule with a Gothic-arched doorway.

In 1962, after weekly Sunday services began, Union Grove became a student-station church, where students at Duke Divinity School served as

Behind the church, an opening leads to a quiet wooded area where 12 benches create a simple amphitheater among the trees.

pastors as part of a university program. Toward the end of the decade, Union Grove was given a full-time ministerial appointment in the North Carolina Conference.

Today, Union Grove Church offers a variety of opportunities for worship and fellowship: traditional services in the stone church, activities in the modern fellowship hall and on the fields behind it, and peaceful worship in the woods.

Concord
UNITED METHODIST CHURCH

NORTHAMPTON COUNTY

CONCORD CHURCH IS THOUGHT to be among the oldest Methodist congregations in North Carolina, but little is known of its early history except what is learned from the first deed. On November 6, 1794, the congregation's seven trustees purchased one acre "whereon a [building] erected for publick worship now stands. . . ." Details are sketchy, although the deed specified that from then on, the site was to be used for Methodist worship only.

Graceful pews line the light-filled sanctuary.

Covered in weatherboards, the one-room Concord Church measures 36 by 40 feet.

The trustees or their successors "shall permit Francis Asbury, Bishop of the Methodist Episcopal Church in America and such other persons as he shall appoint and no other persons to enjoy free use and benefit of the said Premises," the document said. "[They may] preach and expound the Holy Scriptures. . . and when he [Asbury] shall cease to exercise the office of Bishop in the said Methodist Episcopal Church [the trustees] shall at all times forever permit such persons as shall be appointed at the yearly conference of the Methodist Episcopal Church and no other. . . to enjoy the said for the purposes aforesaid. . . ."

It's not known when the present church was built. The congregation generally accepts a mid-1790s construction date, but physical details suggest that either it was built during the mid-19th century or that it was remodeled at that time.

The one-story frame building typifies the simplest form of churches built in North Carolina during the late 18th and 19th centuries. Rectangular and largely plain, these churches had one or two stories and a front-facing gable roof.

Three large sash windows on the side walls and two smaller windows behind the chancel flood the interior with light. Typical of the mid-19th century are the wide-board, flush-sheathed wainscot, the plastered walls, the board-and-batten ceiling, and the Greek Revival–style cornerblock window surrounds. The simple pews, with their gently curving sides, probably also date from this time.

Slow to change, the church used oil lamps that hung by the windows until the 1950s, when they were replaced by electric lights. Likewise, a large wood-burning stove warmed the building until gas heat replaced it in the 1950s. Before an education building was constructed in the 1990s, four Sunday school classes were held in the church—one in each corner of the sanctuary.

Seaboard
UNITED METHODIST CHURCH

SEABOARD,
NORTHAMPTON COUNTY

WITH ITS DARK red brick and bright white trim, "crisp" best describes Seaboard United Methodist Church. Its cross-gable roof and corner tower are typical of many Methodist churches built during the early 20th century in North Carolina. The design likely follows a plan prepared by one of several popular church architects during the last quarter of the 19th century for the Methodist Episcopal Church South, then supplied to the congregation by the denominational office.

Built in the 1920s, Seaboard Church reflects both the Gothic and the Colonial Revival styles. The Gothic Revival predominates and includes the abundance of lancet-arched windows, doors and louvered ventilators. The roof eaves with modillions and cornice returns point to the Colonial Revival.

The sanctuary follows an auditorium plan, in which several sections of pews divided by aisles form a broad curve facing the chancel. A rear wall of folding doors opens to a group of Sunday school rooms. Capitalizing on an economy of

Seaboard's interior typifies many Methodist churches built in North Carolina in the early 20th century.

space, the classrooms can be completely separate from the sanctuary and each other, or open to expand the size of the sanctuary. Large stained-glass windows provide the interior's primary ornamentation. The center windows show biblical scenes with Jesus.

Seaboard United Methodist Church grew out of a community Sunday school held in the railroad station and attended by both Methodists and Baptists.

The Gothic Revival style is seen in the windows, doors and louvered ventilators.

The chancel is set within a recessed arch flanked by two large blind arches.

Land for a house of worship was acquired in 1881, and after meeting for several years in a one-room frame structure, the congregation built a church in 1885. It was demolished in 1922 to make way for the present brick structure. Although built at a cost of $18,000, the new church did not have central heating until 1930, and carpet was not installed until the eve of the dedication on August 25, 1940. The congregation added a two-story education annex in 1958, which continues to be enjoyed by members and community alike.

Carvers Creek
UNITED METHODIST CHURCH

BLADEN COUNTY

CARVERS CREEK is one of the oldest Methodist congregations in North Carolina and the birthplace of Methodism in Bladen County. Francis Asbury, America's first great Methodist evangelist, visited the area three times between 1785 and 1790. By Asbury's last visit, a congregation had been formed.

The Methodists established their place of worship 15 miles southeast of Elizabethtown, on a site that had been used before the Revolutionary War by a group of Quakers. The Quakers left behind a log meeting house, which the Carvers Creek congregation occupied for two decades until a frame church was built. That church burned in 1858, but the present house of worship was built the following year.

In an area that once held prosperous plantations, Carvers Creek Church is large and sophisticated. The difference between it and Trinity Methodist

An expansive cemetery and a dense wood create a picturesque setting for the church.

Carvers Creek was built in 1859 and dedicated the same year.

Church, built a decade earlier in Elizabethtown, is striking. Trinity exhibits a plain, but refined, meeting house form; the Greek Revival temple form of Carvers Creek has a stylishness rarely seen in the area.

Carvers Creek's pedimented portico dominates its weatherboarded exterior. Unusual octagonal columns with molded caps support a full, classical entablature. Sheltered by the portico, two entrances display elongated octagonal panels that echo the columns. Above each entrance is a shuttered

window, and each side of the church has tall windows with five-part louvered shutters.

Inside, a gallery extends around three sides of the sanctuary. The chancel features a communion rail with curvilinear sawnwork balusters and an unusually large, angular pulpit.

Spreading south from the church, a cemetery holds some 500 headstones marking more than two centuries of Methodist burials and 30 unmarked Quaker graves from the mid-18th century.

From 1858 to 1919, Carvers Creek served as the mother church for six Methodist congregations in Bladen Springs, Council, Bolton, Freeman, Delco and East Arcadia. It continues a strong presence in this agricultural region.

Classical posts support the second-floor gallery, which is fronted by a solid, paneled balustrade.

Garber UNITED METHODIST CHURCH

NEW BERN,
CRAVEN COUNTY

GARBER UNITED METHODIST CHURCH reflects the move of the rural church into suburban America. Planned for a community on the outskirts of New Bern and surrounded by new homes and young families, Garber was initially a rural church, though not a farm church. Organized in 1959 with 47 members, the congregation had ballooned to just over 300 members by 1971 when the sanctuary was completed. In the following years, Garber's building program kept pace with congregational growth.

The architecture exhibits the freshness of modern design that was well suited for a postwar growth in church vitality. Of the several one-story, brick-and-stained-wood structures, the sanctuary is the most architecturally interesting. Asymmetry, angles and fine craftsmanship are key to the design prepared by New Bern's Robert H. Stephens. The exterior is a study in angles. The street façade, with its angled planes of differing heights, is crowned with an unusual, openwork spire that rises as a slender cone of metal strips topped with a cross.

Garber's campus is enhanced by a lush, planned landscape with a tree-shaded courtyard that leads to the sanctuary's primary entrance. A low gable with widely overhanging eaves shelters the entrance, while a window wall provides abundant light to the vestibule and eases the transition from the exterior.

Inside the sanctuary, bowed timbers support a lofty cross-gable ceiling. Windows with cross-shaped muntins along the angled side walls hold wavy, translucent glass evocative of swirling water. The chancel emphasizes the fine craftsmanship seen in the church as a whole. Although the altar is centered, the wall behind it is has a highly sophisticated, asymmetrical composition. Positioned within

Garber's interior is a voluminous, modern space where fine craftsmanship rules.

a slight recess, the organ pipes are set in a frame that rises with the ceiling pitch. Above a decorative band of vertical boards is a square, wooden cross surrounded by four painted disks of the symbols for Matthew, Mark, Luke and John. At the rear of the sanctuary, another modern wood cross hangs above the exit. Set on the diagonal beneath the ceiling peak, an abstract stained-glass window depicts a dove descending from God.

The modern design of Garber Church not only recalls the period of its origin, but signals a progressive future for the congregation.

Exterior angles create different perspectives in the play of architectural forms.

FACING: *A cross tops the unusual metal spire.*

Knox Chapel
UNITED METHODIST CHURCH

ROWAN COUNTY

THE OLDEST STANDING Methodist church in Rowan County is also one of the most picturesque. On a small knoll in rolling farmland, Knox Chapel stands back from the road at the head of a circular drive. The cemetery spreads out to its left, and on its right, a one-story, L-shaped education building is attached by a breezeway.

A late example of the 19th-century meetinghouse form, Knox Chapel is a large, rather plain, frame church with a front-gable roof, a square belfry and a gabled entrance porch. Inside, the sanctuary retains its high ceiling, tongue-and-groove wall sheathing, pews with decorative sawnwork ends, communion rail and chancel furnishings.

The Knox Chapel congregation originated in the late 1870s with meetings held near the Knox family farm, possibly under a brush arbor. The Knox family was one of the oldest in Rowan County. Immigrant John Knox acquired the farm's original 600 acres in the mid-18th century, but it grew to nearly

Knox Chapel's peaceful site is bordered by woods.

FACING: *The sanctuary has changed little over the years.*

"One Thing Thou Lackest-Give!"

2,000 acres during the life of his great-grandson, Robert Knox. The congregation was officially organized by 1888, when Robert's son, James, sold the group three acres. They soon began to plan for a permanent house of worship. "Rev. W. L. Dawson, Mooresville Circuit, will soon finish a very large church," announced the Statesville *Landmark* in 1893. "This is a new ground and the membership is large and growing." The church was dedicated six years later. From this auspicious beginning, Knox Chapel has retained a strong presence in its community and a continued association with members of the Knox family—an example of the close ties that often bind religion, family and the land in rural North Carolina.

A partially enclosed stairway leads to a balcony that runs across the back of the sanctuary.

Gibson Memorial
UNITED METHODIST CHURCH

SPRING HOPE,
NASH COUNTY

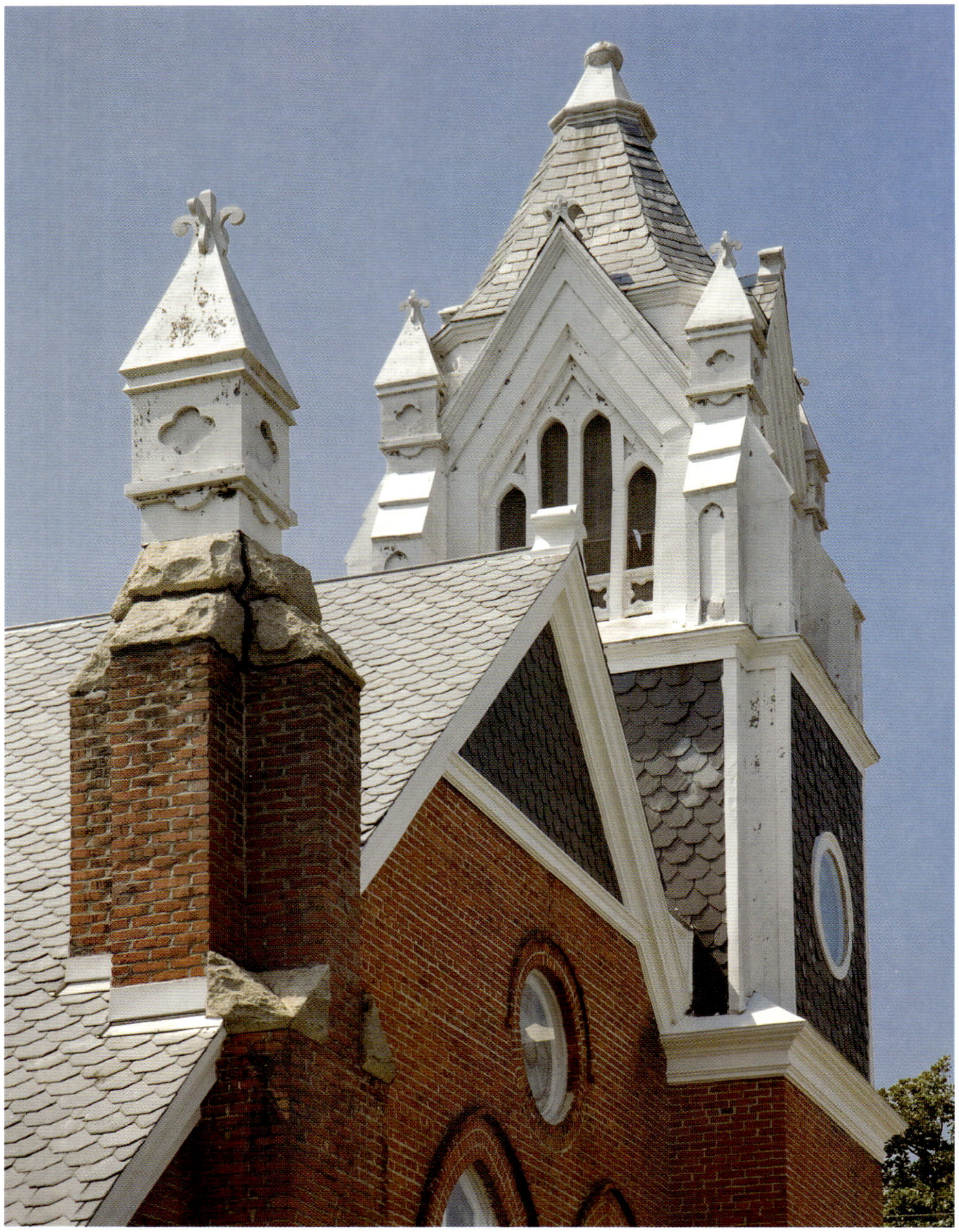

Slate shingles cover the steep roof and decorate the towers and the gable ends.

Like many North Carolina towns in the late 19th and early 20th centuries, Spring Hope began to thrive with the arrival of the railroad. The original community, located about five miles to the southeast, was abandoned as its inhabitants relocated to this booming new railroad town. As Spring Hope prospered, many fine houses, churches and civil and commercial structures were built between the 1890s and World War I. Gibson Memorial Methodist Episcopal Church was among them.

Large stained-glass windows provide colorful relief to the white walls.

SUNDAY SCHOOL 9:45
WORSHIP 11:00
WELCOME!

The predecessor church, Spring Hope Methodist Episcopal, was built at the corner of Nash and Ash streets in the early 1890s. After a fire burned both the church and the parsonage in December 1909, the congregation sold the property and purchased a new lot at Branch and Walnut streets. The cornerstone for the new church—which the congregation renamed Gibson Memorial to honor their first minister—was laid in 1910. Benjamin and Max Price of New Jersey, architects known for their published catalogs of church plans, designed the building.

The exterior of the Gothic Revival–style church features a sophisticated mix of materials and a majestic corner tower. Arched and round stained-glass windows with rough-faced granite sills punctuate the red brick walls. Slate shingles decorate the towers, the gable ends and the steep roof.

Inside, an auditorium-plan sanctuary is set sideways to the front of the church. Pews form a broad curve facing the chancel, which is recessed behind a Tudor arch on the east wall. Typical of the period, dark-stained beaded boards laid in panels cover the high-pitched ceiling. At the south end, folding doors with arched transoms open to what was originally the assembly room (now a chapel) of a simple Akron-plan Sunday school. Its pitched ceiling runs perpendicular to the sanctuary ceiling, but is otherwise identical. Folding doors at the rear of the assembly room originally opened to classrooms. In the 1950s, when growth led to the need for additional space, the congregation added a two-story classroom building, where generations have continued to enjoy years of Christian education and fellowship.

FACING: *The exterior includes a three-stage corner tower and a shorter tower on the west side.*

Madison
UNITED METHODIST CHURCH

MADISON,
ROCKINGHAM COUNTY

MADISON, N.C., WAS ESTABLISHED in 1815 at the confluence of the Dan and Mayo rivers to take advantage of a developing water navigation system. At that strategic location, it became a shipping point for goods from Rockingham and Stokes counties. Prosperity came, and although Madison never grew beyond small-town size, its commercial and cultural links to larger cities brought an awareness of popular architectural styles. Madison became home to many fine buildings.

By the mid-19th century, the Methodists, Presbyterians and Baptists had all built churches in Madison, but Madison Methodist Episcopal Church came first. History says a series of revivals led to its formation; by 1843, church trustees had purchased a half-acre lot on Academy Street and a structure was soon built. Madison's first church was typical of its time—a frame structure with two front doors, clear-glass windows and an upper-level gallery across

Stained-glass windows decorate the sanctuary and flood it with light.

the rear—and it served the congregation until 1909 when a larger facility was needed. The old church was sold and moved across Academy Street, where it stood until 1977.

The building committee for the new church, appointed in March 1909, wasted no time. After hiring contractors from Greensboro, N.C., they chose a design that was probably based on work by architect Benjamin D. Price; the belfry is identical to the one shown in Church Plan 19A of Price's *Catalogue of Architectural Plans for Churches, Parsonages, and Dwelling Houses*, published in Philadelphia in 1885. Workers finished the church in the fall, and the

The interior has curved pews and a floor that slopes toward the chancel.

congregation held its first service on December 12, 1909. "Madison is justly proud of the new Methodist Church," wrote a journalist in 1910.

The red brick building is similar to many other early-20th-century Methodist churches in North Carolina. Madison Church has a cross-gable form with an entrance tower and belfry tucked into the corner where two of the wings meet. The fanciful belfry features decorative pressed-metal shingles. Chamfered corner posts, pierced and sawnwork brackets, and bands of spoolwork decorate the open section that houses the bell.

Inside, the chancel is recessed behind a broad arch. Yellow and green stained-glass windows provide abundant light. The congregation remodeled the sanctuary when an education wing was added in 1954, and the extra space created from the former Sunday school lecture room allowed for more seating on Sunday mornings. In 2007, a larger, more modern structure replaced the entire education building—a testament to the continued growth and vitality of the Madison congregation and its programs.

The focal point for the exterior is the belfry, crowned with a weathervane.

Trinity METHODIST CHURCH

ELIZABETHTOWN,
BLADEN COUNTY

Trinity overlooks East Broad Street in Elizabethtown.

METHODIST BISHOP FRANCIS ASBURY visited Elizabethtown, the Bladen County seat on the Cape Fear River, at least three times in the late 1700s and early 1800s, but a congregation was not organized in the slow-growing town until the mid-1830s.

Bladen County experienced substantial economic growth in the 1840s due to the increased market for turpentine, which was extracted from the area's abundant longleaf pine forests. When a large, two-story frame building was

constructed around 1849 for the church, it reflected the new prosperity enjoyed by the congregation and the town.

Surrounded on three sides by its cemetery, Trinity Methodist Church's visual strength derives from its size and stark simplicity. The gable-front façade is totally plain, and the only exterior decoration is seen in the fancy curvilinear boards covering the upper portion of the square belfry's louvered sides. The center entrance and flanking windows replaced the original pair of front doors in the 1930s.

The white interior is filled with light from 24 windows. Curved pews replaced the original straight ones in the center-aisle sanctuary in the early 20th century, and the classical, pedimented molding on the wall behind the pulpit was added in the 1930s. Classical posts support a paneled gallery that

LEFT: *Classical posts support a paneled gallery.*

RIGHT: *Steep stairs lead to the gallery.*

Large windows line Trinity's sanctuary.

stretches around three sides of the large room. At the rear, the original stair rises steeply to the gallery.

Although the primary place of worship for Trinity's current congregation is its grand 1954 stone building at the corner of West Broad and Marvin streets, special services continue in the old church at the corner of East Broad and Lower streets. Appreciating the historic value of the original building, the congregation has preserved it as Elizabethtown's primary historic landmark.

Franklinton
UNITED METHODIST CHURCH

FRANKLINTON,
FRANKLIN COUNTY

IN 1844, Methodists organized the first religious group in Franklinton, which was one of the first towns in the state to be established because of access to rail service. The congregation took the name Franklinton Methodist Episcopal Church South and constructed a small frame building with a belfry and two front doors. It served until the present church was completed in 1892.

Franklinton Church was designed by prolific Philadelphia architect Benjamin D. Price. Its bricks were made at the state penitentiary and hauled to Franklinton—without cost—by the Seaboard Airline Railroad. Church history says the cornerstone was laid on August 5, 1891, although the date on the

Colorful stained-glass windows decorate the interior.

HYMNAL

stone is July 23, 1891. The first service was held more than a year later and the dedication followed on November 3, 1895.

Designed in the Gothic Revival style, the church's architecture is exceptional. The doors and windows are lancet arched with brick hood molds. A pair of towers of unequal height feature corner pinnacles.

Richly-colored stained-glass windows brighten the sanctuary, and elaborate wood trusses contrast sharply with the white beaded-board ceiling and plastered walls. Roll-up doors with arched stained-glass transoms open from the sanctuary to an Akron-plan Sunday school wing. Although added later, both the doors and the Sunday school were likely part of the original church design that awaited additional funding.

The well-preserved church remains a beautiful structure in this northern North Carolina town.

Bricks for the church were made at the state penitentiary.

FACING: *Inside, pierced X's decorate elaborate wood trusses, and roll-up doors open to the Sunday school.*

AUTHOR'S NOTE

As an architectural historian in North Carolina for 30 years, I have prepared numerous architectural surveys and nominations to the National Register of Historic Places. One of the best aspects of my work is that while I bring much cumulative knowledge to each project, I find that, invariably, I learn something new. As a lifelong learner, this "continuing education" keeps my work exciting. This project on North Carolina's rural Methodist churches did not disappoint.

Having been raised a Baptist and then having spent the last 30 years as an Episcopalian, I found that I had much to learn about the Methodist denomination.

A work of this type is not produced without the advice and assistance of others, and my gratitude in this respect extends to many. I must start with Joe Mann, Charity Perkins, Jeri Krentz and Robb Webb, members of The Duke Endowment staff, whose advice, support and good editing carried the project along. I am grateful, especially, to Joe Mann, whose inspiration for the book turned it from a vision to reality. My thanks also go to the staff of BW&A Books, and particularly to Julie Allred for outstanding design work, prodigious organization skills and for successfully guiding the book to its publication.

Words cannot adequately thank Tim Buchman, photographer extraordinaire, whose great skill and sensitivity created stunning photographs that convey the visual essence of each church.

I am grateful to my colleague and friend, Catherine Bishir, whose support encouraged me from beginning to end, and whose encyclopedic knowledge of North Carolina architecture offered new insights along the way.

Laura Bailey at the North Carolina Conference of the United Methodist Church, Nancy Spaine at the Western North Carolina Conference of the United Methodist Church, the librarians at the Duke University Archives, and the staff of the State Historic Preservation Office all provided willing and able assistance in my research. Bob Jaeger of Partners for Sacred Places and Brian Zuga of Texas Tech University generously shared their thoughts and their research with me. Through them, I gained a broader knowledge of the auditorium and Akron plans and architectural reform in American Protestantism during the 19th and 20th centuries—topics critical to my understanding of the physical character of North Carolina's rural Methodist churches.

NOTES

1. Karen B. Westerfield Tucker, *American Methodist Worship* (New York: Oxford University Press, 2001), 74; Nolan B. Harmon, ed., *The Encyclopedia of World Methodism* (Nashville: United Methodist Publishing House, 1974), 127.
2. Catherine W. Bishir, *North Carolina Architecture*, Portable Edition (Chapel Hill: The University of North Carolina Press, 2005), 214; W. L. Grissom, *History of Methodism in North Carolina, from 1772 to the Present* (Nashville: Publishing House of the M.E. Church, South, 1905), Vol. 1, 329–330; Guion Griffis Johnson, "The Camp Meeting in Ante-Bellum North Carolina," *The North Carolina Historical Review*, Vol. 10, No. 2 (April 1933), 95; Tucker, 75–76, 78.
3. Catawba County Historical Association, *Catawba County: An Architectural History*, Sidney Halma, Project Director (Virginia Beach: The Donning Company/ Publishers, 1991), 14.
4. Tucker, 76.
5. Bishir, 214; Lily Estelle Sigmon, "History and Traditions of Rock Springs Camp Ground," Rock Springs Camp Meeting, 144th Annual Session, August 4–12, 1973, Denver, N.C., 10, 12; Johnson, 96.
6. Harmon, 126–127.
7. Harmon, 127.
8. Joshua Leigh, "On Church Building," 10 April 1834, Church Book, Iredell Circuit (United Methodist Church Records, 1784–1974 and undated, North Carolina Conference Series: Circuit, Charge and Church Records Subseries—Iredell Co., Lincoln Co., Box NCC49, Rare Book, Manuscript and Special Collections Library, Duke University), 2–11.
9. Leigh, 6–11.
10. Bishir, 218, 222, 227–228; Tucker, 239.
11. Bishir, 370–371.
12. Brian Christopher Zugay, "Towards a 'New Era' in Church Building: Architectural Reform in American Protestantism in the Nineteenth and Early-Twentieth Centuries," Ph.D. diss., Brown University, 2004, 4, 74.
13. Zugay, 147–149, 182; A. Robert Jaeger, "The Auditorium and Akron Plans: Reflections of a Half Century of American Protestantism," Master's Thesis, Cornell University, 1984, 85.
14. Zugay, 191–192.
15. Zugay, 234, 236; Jaeger, 73–82.
16. Zugay, 236–237; Bishir, 379.

17. Zugay, 238.
18. Tucker, 248; Jaeger, 131.
19. Zugay, 237–238; Jaeger, 132, 137.
20. Jaeger, 138.
21. Zugay, 240–241; Jaeger, 141, 146–147, 151, 164; Bishir, 382, 384.
22. Jaeger, 161.
23. Zugay, 241–242, 249; Jaeger, 173, 176.
24. Tucker, 252.
25. Tucker, 252–254.
26. Robert F. Durden, *Lasting Legacy to the Carolinas: The Duke Endowment, 1924–1994* (Durham: Duke University Press, 1998), 167.
27. Zugay, 327; Durden, 168, 174, 176; "Important Announcement by Dr. Few," *North Carolina Christian Advocate,* 8 August 1929; "Architect Will Aid Churches in Country," *Greensboro Daily News,* 10 August 1929.
28. Tucker, 253.
29. Tucker, 255.